JOHN BULL, 1580

From a painting belonging to the Faculty of Music, Oxford

THE
FIRST BOOK OF THE
GREAT
MUSICIANS

A Course in Appreciation for
Young Readers

BY

PERCY A. SCHOLES

TENTH EDITION

LONDON
OXFORD UNIVERSITY PRESS
NEW YORK   TORONTO

Oxford University Press, Ely House, London W. 1

GLASCOW NEW YORK TORONTO MELBOURNE WELLINGTON
CAPE TOWN IBADAN NAIROBI DAR ES SALAAM LUSAKA ADDIS ABABA
DELHI BOMBAY CALCUTTA MADRAS KARACHI LAHORE DACCA
KUALA LUMPUR SINGAPORE HONG KONG TOKYO

First edition	*1920*
Tenth edition	*1942*
Sixteenth impression	*1974*

Printed in Great Britain by
The Camelot Press Ltd., London and Southampton

CONTENTS

LIST OF ILLUSTRATIONS

NOTE

FOR TEACHERS AND PARENTS

THE composers treated in this First Book of the Great Musicians have been chosen in such a way as to illustrate the whole course of development of music from the sixteenth century to the twentieth. Many important composers are, of course, left over for the Second and Third Books, which also include chapters on the Pianoforte and the Organ, a fuller description of the orchestra, and one of the Military Band, and a sketch of the subjects of Oratorio and Opera. These Second and Third Books are written in a style suitable for slightly older readers.

NOTE TO THE THIRD EDITION

THE Author wishes to call attention to the fact that the whole plan of his book (with its designedly intimate style and its many pictorial, diagrammatic and musical illustrations) has been dictated by the intention that *it should actually lie under the eyes of the children themselves*. He believes that where, in the class teaching of Musical Appreciation, his chapters are merely read to the class, or their matter re-told, instead of their being read *by the class*, a good deal of the impression he has wished to leave on the minds of the children must be lost. He hopes, too, that, in addition to class use, the book may be of some service in the hands of young pianoforte and violin pupils—whose lessons are necessarily too short to allow of much direct treatment of the appreciative side of the art they are learning.

TO THE READER

IF you want to play a good game at cricket or football or tennis you have to *learn* how the game is played, and to *practise* it. When you have learnt and practised, then you get the enjoyment.

And, in the same way, if you want to listen properly to lots of the very best music you have to *learn* about it and then to *practise* listening. And, here again, when you have learnt and practised you get the enjoyment.

But learning about a game, and practising it, are really quite good fun in themselves.

And I hope you will find that learning about music, and practising listening to it, are also good quite fun in themselves.

If you don't get some fun out of this book as you study it, and then, when you have studied it, get greater enjoyment out of listening to music, you will greatly disappoint—

THE AUTHOR.

PORTRAIT GALLERY OF GREAT MUSICIANS

CATALOGUE

HENRY PURCELL
Reproduced by kind permission from a painting by Sir Godfrey Kneller, in the National Portrait Gallery

GEORGE FREDERICK HANDEL
From a painting by Sir James Thornhill in the Fitzwilliam Museum, Cambridge

JOHN SEBASTIAN BACH
From a print in the British Museum

JOSEPH HAYDN
From an old print

MOZART, AGED 7, WITH HIS SISTER AND FATHER
From a drawing by L. C. de Carmontelle, 1763

BEETHOVEN
Reproduced by kind permission from a drawing in the possession of the Royal College of Music

ROBERT SCHUMANN
From a drawing by A. Menzel

FREDERIC CHOPIN
From a drawing by Rudolph Lehmann, 1847, in the Print-room, British Museum

EDWARD GRIEG
From a painting by Eilif Peterssen in the National Gallery, Oslo
By kind permission of the Artist

SIR EDWARD ELGAR
From a drawing by Will Rothenstein
By kind permission of the Artist

EDWARD MACDOWELL
From a photograph
By kind permission of Messrs. Elkin & Co., Ltd.

HENRY PURCELL

From a painting by Sir Godfrey Kneller, in the
National Portrait Gallery

GEORGE FREDERICK HANDEL

From a painting by Sir James Thornhill in the
Fitzwilliam Museum, Cambridge

JOHN SEBASTIAN BACH

From a print in the British Museum

JOSEPH HAYDN

From an old print

MOZART, AGED 7, WITH HIS SISTER AND FATHER

From a drawing by L. C. de Carmontelle, 1763

BEETHOVEN

From a drawing in the possession of the Royal College of Music

ROBERT SCHUMANN

From a drawing by A. Menzel

FREDERIC CHOPIN

From a drawing by Rudolph Lehmann, 1847

EDWARD GRIEG

From a painting by Eilif Peterssen in the National Gallery, Oslo

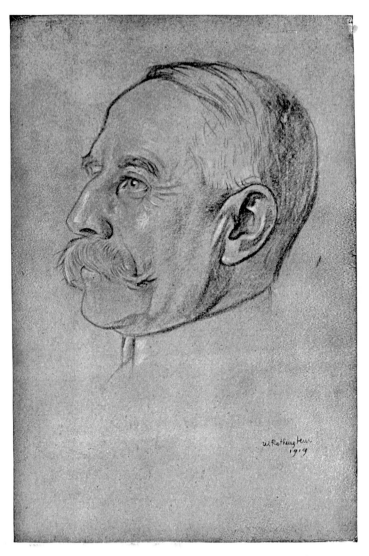

SIR EDWARD ELGAR

From a drawing by Will Rothenstein

EDWARD MACDOWELL

From a photograph

I

THE COUNTRY PEOPLE AS COMPOSERS

A CHAPTER ON FOLK MUSIC

THIS is a book about the Great Composers—by which we generally mean men of musical genius, who have had a long training in music, and learnt how to make beautiful songs and long fine pieces for piano, or orchestra, or chorus. But these are not the only composers.

It is not so difficult to compose little tunes as people think, and if you keep your ears open you will often find people composing without knowing they are doing it. For instance, if a boy has to call 'evening paper' over and over again in the street, night after night, you will find that he turns it into a little four-note song. Notice this and try to write down his song next time you hear it. Little children of two years old croon to themselves tiny tunes they have made up without knowing it. It would surprise their mothers if you told them their babies were composers—but they are!

And in all countries the simple country people, who have had no musical training, have yet made up very charming music—songs or dance tunes, or tunes for playing games. Music such as this we call FOLK MUSIC.

A Folk Tune is never very long or difficult, and it is only a 'Melody' (that is, it is only a single line of notes, without any accompaniment). But, in their simple style, the Folk Tunes are very beautiful, and no composer can make anything better than the best of them.

Just in the same way you will find that the country people in every land have Folk Tales and often Folk Plays—so they are not only composers, but authors and playwrights too.

Work Music, Play Music, and Religious Music.

Some of the Folk Tunes are a part of children's games which have come down for centuries. Others are a help in work, such as rowing songs (to help the rowers to keep time with their oars), songs to be sung while milking, and so on. Others, again, are part of the religion—Folk Carols to sing at Christmas from house to house, and songs and dances belonging to far-off times, before Christianity, when people thought they had to sing and dance to welcome the Sun God when he reappeared in spring; such pagan dances and songs as these latter still go on in some places, though people have forgotten their full meaning. Then, of course, there are love songs, hunting songs, and drinking songs, and songs about pirates and highwaymen, songs about going to the wars, and sea songs. There are songs on all manner of subjects in fact, for everything that interested the country people was put into songs.

How Nations express their Feelings in Music.

You cannot imagine a sad baby making up happy little tunes, can you? Or a happy baby making sad ones? And so with nations—their general character comes out in their songs. And every nation gets into its own particular way of making its tunes, so as to express its various feelings. English tunes are generally different from Scottish tunes, Irish from Welsh, and so forth. You can generally tell one of the negro songs from the Southern States when you hear it, and nobody who has heard much Folk Music of various nations is likely to hear a Norwegian song and think it an Italian or French one.

Collecting Tunes—a useful Hobby.

The trouble is that the country people are now hearing so many of the town-made tunes, that come to them in cheap music books or as gramophone records, that they are quickly forgetting their own old country songs. So some musicians have made a hobby of collecting the Folk Tunes before they get lost. They go out with note-book and pencil, and get the older folks to sing them the tunes that were sung in the villages when they were boys and girls, and where the old Folk Dances are still used they manage to see these, and to copy down the music of the fiddler and the steps of the dance. So much of the Folk Music is being saved (only just in time!), and some of it is now printed and taught in schools, so that it may be handed down by the children to coming generations.

In America, where so many races mingle, you can collect Folk Music of all nations. In the Southern Appalachian mountains, where the people are descended from British settlers of long ago and have not mingled much with other people because the mountains cut them off, the Folk Songs are still much the same as you find in England and Scotland. You can collect lots of Irish tunes in other parts of America, and Russian, and German, and Hungarian, and Italian tunes. In addition there are, of course, negro tunes (partly descended from African melodies) and American Indian tunes.

How Folk Songs have influenced Composers.

In all the countries the skilled and trained composers have at times used Folk Songs as parts of their larger pieces. How they do this you will learn later in the book. And the 'Form' or shape of the Folk Tunes have shown composers how to form or shape their big piano and orchestral pieces. It will help us in our study of the big works of the great composers if we can come to understand the little tunes of the people.

The thing to do is to play or sing a Folk Tune and then find out how it is made up. For instance, if we take this little North of England song and examine it we shall learn a good deal.

BARBARA ALLEN

II.

Here you see is a tune that falls into two parts, balancing one another, so to speak. We might call it a 'two-bit tune' (inventing a useful word).

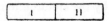

Now we will take another tune; this time it happens to be a Welsh one.

ALL THRO' THE NIGHT

There you see is a strain (I) which comes at the beginning and end of the song, and in between, for the sake of variety, another strain (II). We might call that a 'three-bit tune', or (if you like) a 'sandwich tune'. There are lots of tunes we can call by that name. You see what it means—don't you?

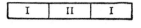

QUESTIONS

(TO SEE WHETHER YOU REMEMBER THE CHAPTER AND UNDERSTAND IT)

1. If somebody said to you 'Can you tell me what is meant by the words "Folk Music"?' what would you reply?

2. What do we mean by a 'melody'?

3. Mention some of the different subjects of the songs sung by the country-folk.

4. What should we mean if we said 'a nation's heart is seen in its songs'?

5. Which do you think is the most useful hobby: (1) collecting foreign stamps, (2) collecting bird's eggs, or (3) collecting Folk Tunes, and why do you think so? (Do not be afraid of saying what *you* really think.)

6. Say two ways in which skilled composers have got help from the music of simple folk.

THINGS TO DO

(FOR SCHOOL AND HOME)

1. Play, or get somebody to play for you, a lot of Folk Tunes from some song book, and find out how each tune is made. You will find a great many of them are either in the two bits (I–II) or the three bits (I–II–I). This exercise is important: it will teach you how to listen.

2. Get into your head as many good Folk Tunes as you can, so that you will always have something jolly to sing or whistle. This will help to make you musical. Some of the country people in England know as many as 300 or 400 old tunes. How many can *you* learn and remember?

3. Play or listen to a good many Scottish tunes, and see if you can find out from them what sort of people the Scots people are. Then do the same with the tunes of the English, Irish, Welsh, or any other nation.

4. Get somebody to teach you a Folk Dance, or, if you cannot do this, make up your own little dance to one of the Folk Tunes in a song book.

5. Find a really interesting Folk Song that tells a story and then get some friends to act it with you, whilst someone sings the song. Dressing up will help to make this enjoyable.

6. Find a good Folk Tune with a marching or dancing swing; let one play it on the piano whilst the others put in a note here and there on glasses tapped with spoons, and any other domestic orchestral instruments of the kind. Some can also play the tune on combs with paper. (Glasses can be made to sound particular notes by putting more or less water in them.)

7. Discover any other ways of getting some fun out of Folk Tunes and learning a lot of them.

BRITONS AND BRETONS

THE STORY OF A THOUSAND-YEAR-OLD SONG

In 1758 a British force landed in France—at St. Cast, in Brittany. A Breton regiment was marching to meet it when all at once it stopped—*the British soldiers were singing one of its own Breton national songs!* The Bretons, carried away by their feelings, joined in the refrain. The officers on each side told their men to fire—and the words of command were found to be in the same language. Instead of firing at each other, the two forces threw down their weapons and became friends.

How was this? The British regiment was Welsh, and the Welsh are descendants of the ancient Britons—driven into the mountains of Wales by the Saxons in the sixth century, at the same time as the ancestors of the Bretons were driven across the sea into Brittany.

After more than a thousand years, the descendants of these two bodies of the old British nation met, and found they knew the same language and the same songs. Differences had crept into the language and into the songs, of course, but the two regiments could talk together without much difficulty, and join in the Chorus together.

This shows how people cling to their national songs. This one is now known in Brittany as *Emgann Sant-Kast* (The Battle of St. Cast) and is still popular in Wales as *Captain Morgan's March.* It can be found in some song books.[1]

[1] e.g. *Welsh Melodies*, published by Boosey & Co.

ENGLISH MUSIC IN THE DAYS OF DRAKE AND SHAKESPEARE

A CHAPTER ON THE BEGINNING OF MODERN MUSIC

An Explorer and his Music.

When Francis Drake set out on his expedition round the world in 1577, tiny though the ship was, he yet found room in it for *musicians*. You would imagine that he would use all his little space for sailors and soldiers; but it was not so, and at meal-times he always had the musicians play before him. A Spanish admiral whom he took prisoner and whose diary has lately been printed says 'the Dragon' (for that was what the Spaniards called Drake) 'always dined and supped to the music of viols'.

The music of Drake and his men always interested the savages wherever they went. When the ship approached one island the king came off in a canoe to meet them, with six grave old counsellors with him. The ship's boat was towing at the stern and the king made signs asking that the band whose music he heard might get into the boat; then he fastened his canoe to the boat and was towed along in that way, and (says Drake's chaplain, who wrote the story of the voyage) for an hour the king was 'in musical paradise'.

Drake's crew were great singers, and when they went on shore in another place, and built a fort to stay in for a time, the savages used to come to hear them sing their psalms and hymns at the time of prayers. 'Yea, they took such pleasure in our singing of Psalms, that whensoever they resorted to us, their first request was commonly this, Gnaah, by which they entreated that we should sing.'

If you read the chaplain's book, *The World Encompassed*, you will find many other little stories that will show you how musical were Drake and his seamen, or, if you prefer a modern tale book about Drake, Kingsley's *Westward Ho!* will tell you much the same.

So much for an Elizabethan explorer. Now for an actor and author.

A Dramatist and his Music.

In those days the Stratford boy William Shakespeare was in London and had become a famous writer of plays. He must have been very fond of music, for we find he brings it into almost everything he writes. When he wants to make his audience believe in fairies (as in *A Midsummer-Night's Dream*) he has music—pretty little fairy songs. And when he wants to make people realize how horrible witches are (as in *Macbeth*) he has grim witch songs. His mad people (like King Lear) sing little, disordered snatches of song in a mad sort of way. His drunken people sing bits of songs in a riotous way. His people in love sing sentimental songs.

When Shakespeare wants to represent a vision of any sort (as when Queen Katharine is about to die, in *Henry VIII*) he prepares the feelings of his audience by music. Whenever a marvellous cure is to be performed (as in *King Lear* and other plays) he has music. When there is fighting he has trumpets and drums, and when there is a funeral procession he has a Dead March.

There is much more music in Shakespeare than this, but enough has been said to show you how musical was that writer of plays and how musical must have been the audience for whom he wrote the plays. Because of course he wrote what he knew people would like.

A Queen and her Music.

Once when an ambassador from Queen Mary of Scotland came to the court of Queen Elizabeth of England, one of the

courtiers took him into a room and hid him behind the arras
so that he might hear the Queen play the VIRGINALS (a sort of
keyboard instrument, something like a small piano).[1] The
courtier told him to be very quiet as the Queen would be
angry if she knew. But the Scotsman pulled the arras aside,
and the Queen saw him. She seemed very angry with him
for taking such a liberty, so he fell on his knees and begged to
be forgiven. Then the Queen asked him—'Which is the
better player, the Queen of Scotland or the Queen of
England?' and of course he had to say 'The Queen of
England'. As he did so he saw, of course, that his being
taken to hear the Queen had really been at her command, so
that she could ask this question.

So queens played in those days and were proud of their
playing.

Everybody Musical Then.

In those days everybody seems to have been musical. The
common people sang their Folk Songs and their Rounds and
Catches. The rich people and courtiers sang a sort of part-
song called a MADRIGAL, and if you went out to supper it was
taken as a matter of course that when the madrigal books were
brought out you could sing your part at sight.

There were many musical instruments such as the
Virginals (mentioned above), small Organs in churches, Viols
(big and little instruments of the violin kind to play together
in sets), Recorders (a kind of flute, big and little, also playing
together in sets), Lutes (something like mandolines), and
Hautboys (oboes), Trumpets, and Drums, for military and
other purposes.

Choral Music.

The choral singing was very famous then. It was so made
that every voice or part (Treble, Alto, Tenor, and Bass) had
a beautiful melody to sing, and yet all these beautiful

[1] See p. 37 [footnote].

melodies put together made a beautiful piece of music. There were lovely Anthems in the churches, made in this way.

The ROUNDS and CATCHES mentioned above were pieces where all the three or four voices sang the same melody, but beginning one after another, and the melody had to be carefully made so as to fit with itself when sung in this way. *You* can sing Catches; they are very good fun. A Round and a Catch are almost the same thing. We might say that when a Round has funny words we call it a Catch. *Three Blind Mice* is an Elizabethan catch.

Keyboard Music.

The English composers led the world at that time in writing for the Virginals. They showed how to write music that was not just like the choral music, but was really suited for fingers on a keyboard. All the piano music of the great composers may be said to have sprung from the English virginal music of the sixteenth century. The Elizabethan composers laid the foundation, and Bach and Beethoven and Chopin and others have built upon it.

Form in Instrumental Music.

When discussing Folk Songs we learnt a little about Form. In Queen Elizabeth's day composers were trying to find out good 'forms' for instrumental music.

One form they found was the VARIATIONS form. They would take some jolly tune (perhaps a popular Folk Tune), and write it out simply; then they would write it again with elaborations, and then again with further elaborations, and so on to the end. All the great composers down to our own day have been fond of the Variations form, and it was the English Elizabethan composers who invented it.

Another form was made by writing two little pieces in the style of the dances of the day and playing them one after the other, to make a longer piece. Generally one was a slow, stately dance called a Pavane, and the other a quick, nimble dance, called a Galliard.

The Fame of English Musicians.

In these days English musicians were famous all over Europe, and were often sent for by the princes and kings of various countries to be attached to their courts. One called John Dowland became the King of Denmark's lute player and composer, and his music was printed in many European cities. Another, with the truly English name of John Bull, became organist of Antwerp Cathedral. A very famous composer of choral and virginal music in these days was William Byrd, and another was Orlando Gibbons. Try to remember the names of these men and to hear some of their music

QUESTIONS

(TO SEE WHETHER YOU REMEMBER THE CHAPTER
AND UNDERSTAND IT)

1. What do you know of Drake and his music?
2. What do you know of Shakespeare and his music?
3. Tell a story about Queen Elizabeth and music.
4. What was the virginals like?
5. What were the viols?
6. What is the difference between a lute and a flute?
7. Mention a kind of flute common in the sixteenth century.
8. What is a Madrigal?
9. What is a Round?
10. What is a Catch? Do you know one?
11. How did English composers lay the foundation of modern piano music (two ways, please!)?
12. Describe 'Variations'.
13. Describe a form which consisted of dance tunes.
14. Mention four great English musicians of Shakespeare's day.

THINGS TO DO

1. Get two of your friends to learn this Catch with you. (It is quite easy.) Sir Toby, Sir Andrew, and the Clown sing it in *Twelfth Night*.

QUARRELLING CATCH

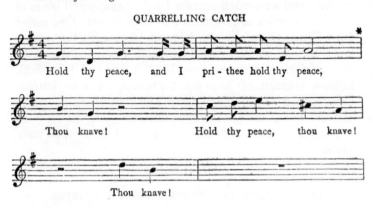

At first practise it, all singing the same notes, as though it were an ordinary song. Count the rests carefully and sing firmly.

Then sing it this way—first singer begins and when he gets to the mark * second singer begins, and when *he* gets to * third singer begins. Now all three are singing, but each treading on the tail of the one before, so to speak.

When the leader has sung the Catch about five times through he gives a sign and all stop together, or better, as this is a quarrelling Catch, after going through three or four times, shaking fists at each other, you can fall to fighting and so stop.

2. Then (for a change) practise this quieter Round of Shakespeare's day. Here some occasional soft singing will be in place. Try various ways of arranging soft and loud passages, with *crescendos* and *diminuendos* and settle on the way that sounds best.

CHURCH-GOING CATCH

All in - to ser - vice

Let us sing mer - ri - ly to - geth -

- er, Ding dong ding dong bell.

3. Now practise *Three Blind Mice* in the same way.

4. Play this Elizabethan hymn tune on the piano:

Glory to thee, my God, this night
For all the blessings of the light;
Keep me, O keep me, King of kings,
Beneath thy own almighty wings.

Forgive me, Lord, for thy dear Son,
The ill that I this day have done,
That with the world, myself, and thee,
I, ere I sleep, at peace may be.

You see that this tune has parts for four voices—Treble and Alto (on the top stave), and Tenor and Bass (on the bottom stave). Play or sing the Tenor by itself. Have you discovered anything?

Now perform the tune in this way. Get a friend to play it on the piano. You sing the Treble and get some grown-up male person to sing the Tenor.

This tune is called *Tallis's Canon*. Tallis was a great composer in Queen Elizabeth's reign. A CANON (as you have now discovered) is a piece in which one voice sings the same as another, but a few beats after it. We say that these two voices are 'singing in Canon'. In your Catches *all* the voices were 'singing in Canon'.

5. Go through any Shakespeare play that you know and find any allusions to music. Where Shakespeare means music to be performed in the play, see if you can find out why he does so.

6. If possible, get some grown-up or other good pianist to play you a piece in Variations form belonging to the Elizabethan times, for example:

> John Bull's *The King's Hunting Jig*.
> Orlando Gibbons's *The Queen's Command*.
> Giles Farnaby's *Pawle's Wharfe*.

Get them played several times and listen carefully, so as to find out how the tune is changed in each of the Variations.

7. In the same way get someone to play some of the other Elizabethan Virginals music. Giles Farnaby's is perhaps most likely to please you—especially when you get used to it (of course it is in a different style from the music of to-day, so may take a little getting used to).

He has one little piece called *Giles Farnaby's Dreame* (what sort of a dream was it that suggested this piece to him?) and another called *His Rest*, where you can feel him falling asleep. You can find bits of Canon in *His Rest*: try to hear these as the piece is played.

Then there is a bright little piece called *Giles Farnaby's Conceit* ('conceit' in those days simply meant a bright idea), and another called *His Humour* ('humour' then meant character or temperament).

So in his music Farnaby used often to picture himself. Judging by these pictures, what sort of a man do you think he was? Listen to them carefully several times, and then make up your mind.

DIAGRAMS

1. TALLIS'S CANON

Treble

Alto

Tenor

Bass

The straight lines show the two parts that are written in Canon. The wavy lines show the parts which just go on their ordinary way, not in Canon (we call these 'free parts'). The arrow points show where the melody begins.

2. A ROUND IN THREE PARTS

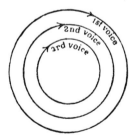

It is a very good plan to make diagrams of the pieces you sing and play and hear, because it helps you to grasp how they are made, and so to understand and enjoy them better.

III

HENRY PURCELL

ON a certain Tuesday afternoon in the month of February, 1660, four men sat before the fire in a Coffee House in Westminster. One was called Pepys, another Locke, another was a Captain Taylor, and the last was a Mr. Purcell.

There they sat chatting, and if you think for a few minutes of what you have read in your history books as occurring at that time you will be able to guess what it was they were discussing so eagerly as they sipped their coffee. What happened at the beginning of the year 1660? Why! *the King came back again!*

That is what excited them so much. The Long Parliament had been recalled and it had been decided to ask Charles to return.

'Look!' said Pepys suddenly, pointing at the window, and turning round they saw the glare of bonfires all along the river banks. The city was soon ablaze with flames. 'Listen!' said Captain Taylor, and as they did so they heard bells beginning to ring: the bells of St. Clement's, and the bells of St. Martin's, and the bells of Old Bailey, and the bells of Shoreditch, the bells of Stepney, the bells of Old Bow, and, deep below them all, the big booming bells of Westminster Abbey and Old St. Paul's—soon they were all clanging and jangling together.

How they sang Songs for Joy.

Then some more friends came into the room, and they all began to sing. Locke and Purcell, who were both musicians,

sang some Italian and Spanish songs, and Pepys struck up a
tune too. And by and by Mr. Locke pulled out of his
pocket a fine piece of music he had made as soon as he heard
that the King was likely to come in again. It was a 'Canon'
for eight voices, with Latin words, *Domine salvum fac Regem.*

So Locke taught them the tune and they all sat round the
fire in their high-backed chairs, and one after another, at a
sign from the composer, they began to sing the words
Domine salvum, until they were all singing merrily together.

When Pepys got home that night he took down a little book
in which he was accustomed to write his diary, and wrote his
account of the day's doings, and how he had gone to the
Coffee House, and seen the fires and heard the bells. '*It was a
most pleasant sight*', he wrote, '*to see the city from one end to the
other with a glory about it, so bright was the light of the bonfires,
and so thick round the city, and the bells rang everywhere.*'

Why Mr. Purcell rejoiced.

Now when Mr. Purcell got home (he had not far to go, for
he lived in Westminster) you may be sure he told his good
wife all about his doings, and it is certain that they both
remembered one special reason for rejoicing that the King
was coming back.

You see Mr. Purcell was a musician—one of the best in
London. Now, whilst the Puritans were in power there had
been no Church Music. Mr. Purcell had probably earned
money by singing in the Opera[1] and at private houses, and by
teaching young ladies to play the harpsichord[2] or teaching
men to sing. But with the King would come back the old
Church ways, and that meant anthems and choirs and organs.
The Puritans liked music—but not in Church. The only
music they allowed in church was plain psalm-singing by all
the congregation—no organs and no choirs. Mr. Purcell
loved anthems and other Church music, and knew that it was

[1] An Opera is a play set to music.   [2] See p. 37.

very likely that now his fine voice would earn him a good position in some choir. Besides he had a little baby son, and he may have had a fancy that he would in a few years make him a choirboy, and so get him a good musical training.

This chapter is really about the baby son, for he became the greatest British composer. But first it must be said that when the King came back and the music began again in the Chapel Royal, Mr. Purcell was chosen to be a member of the choir, as well as later being given some other musical positions at Court, so he was now very happy.

Purcell becomes a Choirboy.

When little Henry was old enough he was admitted as a choirboy in the Chapel Royal. So every Sunday, with the other boys and men, he sang before the King. In Purcell's day they had not only the organ, but also four-and-twenty fiddlers, for the King loved the sound of stringed instruments, and as soon as he had returned had set up a band like that which he had heard at the Court of France.

So for some years young Henry sang in the King's choir and in his leisure time practised the harpsichord and organ, and, no doubt, the violin also. And besides all that he soon began to compose. When he was twelve he was chosen, as the cleverest of the choirboys, to write a piece of music as a birthday present for the King. It was called *The Address of the Children of the Chapel Royal to the King on his Majesty's Birthday*, A.D. 1670.

Purcell's Voice breaks.

Purcell's voice broke when he was fifteen or sixteen, but they kept him on at the chapel for a time, perhaps making use of him for some odd jobs, such as teaching the younger boys. Then the Westminster Abbey authorities gave him some work as music-copyist. And by and by some of the theatre managers heard what a good composer he was, and asked him to write music for their plays. So he soon began to be quite busy.

Organist of the Abbey and the Chapel Royal.

Purcell was now becoming famous, and when he was about twenty-one a wonderful thing happened. Dr. Blow, the organist of Westminster Abbey, seeing how clever Purcell was, offered to resign so that Purcell might take his place.

Purcell must have been grateful to Dr. Blow, for now, as Abbey organist, he had a big enough income to marry a girl of whom he had become very fond. So in a little house in Westminster Purcell settled down. Later the King made him organist of the Chapel Royal. Now he held two great positions and had become the most important musical man in England, and you may be sure that his young wife was very proud of him.

Purcell's Compositions.

All this time Purcell was very busy composing. He composed a great deal of church music—Anthems and Services for Westminster Abbey and the Chapel Royal. Some of the Anthems are very solemn, and those, I believe, were for Westminster Abbey. And others were quite gay; probably these were for the Chapel Royal, for Charles II loved jolly music, even in church.

For the Violin he wrote one piece—a wonderful Sonata— which was discovered only a few years ago.

Purcell also wrote a lot of lovely music for two Violins with one 'Cello and a Harpsichord. This music is very much neglected, which is a great pity.

Besides all this, Purcell wrote a good deal of music for the theatres, and when you hear a Purcell song, such as *Full Fathom Five*, or *Come if you dare*, or *Nymphs and Shepherds*, or *Come unto these Yellow Sands*, you are generally listening to one of Purcell's theatre pieces.

There are, too, some lovely sacred songs that singers to-day neglect frightfully—to their great disgrace.

Purcell's Kings and Queens.

When Charles II died Purcell went on being royal organist, and so became a servant of James II. And when James II was turned out of the country, Purcell became organist to William and Mary. So he was royal organist in three reigns.

One of his tasks was to write 'Odes', or complimentary verses set to music, whenever anything happened in the Royal Family. For instance, when the King came back to London from his holidays, he would be welcomed with the performance of an Ode, for solo voices and chorus and orchestra. And Purcell would sit at the Harpsichord and lead the music.

He also had to play at two Coronations in Westminster Abbey, and at the funeral of Queen Mary.

Purcell's Death.

It is a sad thing that the greatest British composer died when he was only thirty-seven years of age. Who knows what he might have done if he had lived twenty or thirty years longer?

The Form of Purcell's Music.

If you take any little harpsichord piece of Purcell's and play it on the piano you will generally find that its form is like that of *Barbara Allen* and similar folk songs (p. 3). That is to say, it falls into two strains; in other words, it is a two-bit tune—or, to use the proper term, it is in BINARY FORM. You can find a sort of half-way house in the middle, where we have a CADENCE—that is, a sort of ear-resting place. Then the piece starts again, and we come to the end of the journey with another Cadence. Another word for Cadence is 'Close'.

It has already been said that the Elizabethan Composers

often strung two little pieces together to make one longer piece. Purcell went farther than this, and often strung three or four little pieces into one. Such a string of pieces we call a SUITE. Generally these little pieces were all in the style of the dances of the day, except the first piece, which was a PRELUDE, the word 'Prelude' simply meaning an opening piece.

Purcell for some reason does not seem to have cared much for the Air and Variations of which the Elizabethans were so fond. But he sometimes wrote what we might call a Bass with Variations, in which the same little bit of bass comes over and over again, with the tune above it changed every time. This we call a GROUND BASS, or simply GROUND. Some of his songs and some of his Harpsichord pieces are written in this way.

Some of Purcell's songs have a piece of RECITATIVE before them—that is, a piece of singing which does not make much of a tune, but imitates the way in which one would recite the words in a dramatic performance.

QUESTIONS

(TO SEE WHETHER YOU REMEMBER THE CHAPTER AND UNDERSTAND IT)

1. How many historical events can you remember which will fix in your mind the time when Purcell lived? How old was Purcell when the Plague of London happened?—And the Fire?

2. What do you know of Purcell's father?

3. What sort of music do you think Cromwell liked in church? And what sort did Charles II like?

4. In what church was Purcell a choirboy? And in what churches was he organist?

5. How old was Purcell when he died?

6. Mention any instruments for which Purcell wrote music.

7. What is a Cadence? Give another name for it.
8. What is Binary Form?
9. What is a Suite?
10. What is a Prelude?
11. What is a Ground Bass?
12. What is a Recitative?

THINGS TO DO

1. Learn one of Purcell's songs. (*Come if you dare!* and *Britons strike Home* are bold songs, and *Full Fathom Five* and *Come unto these Yellow Sands* are gentler songs. All are quite jolly and they cost very little if you get them in a school singing-class edition. *Full Fathom Five* and *Come unto these Yellow Sands* are settings of words in Shakespeare's *The Tempest*. You might turn up the play, if you like, and find out just how they come in.)

2. Get somebody to play a few of Purcell's Harpsichord pieces, and when you feel the middle Cadence has come, call out 'half-time'. Have each piece played several times and try to notice as much as possible how the piece is made. Some pieces are made almost entirely of one little group of four or five notes, over and over again, sometimes high and sometimes low. And in some pieces you can find bits of IMITATION—that is, one 'part' or 'voice' giving out a little bit of tune and another answering it. Most of the instrumental music by Purcell (like most of the Elizabethan music) is in 'voices' or separate little strands of melody woven together, almost as though (say) a Treble and Tenor and Bass were singing it.

3. If you are a pianist, practise some of Purcell's music for Harpsichord.

4. If you play the fiddle you can buy some little tunes of Purcell which have been arranged for that instrument, and practise them.

5. If you have a School Orchestra get it to play some of the Purcell tunes that have been arranged for stringed instruments.

6. You could make up a dance to some of the Purcell music. For instance, you could dance to the song *Come unto these Yellow Sands*, the words of which are about dancing on the beach.

7. Make a little play of Purcell and his wife giving a little party to celebrate the coronation of William and Mary and have some of his music performed as a part of the play.

8. Look out for any Purcell music in the broadcast programmes and in *The Radio Times*, and when you find any, make a note of the day and time, so as not to miss it.

9. When buying Gramophone Records, ask the dealer what Purcell records he has got, or can get for you.

IV

GEORGE FREDERICK HANDEL
1685–1759

How he practised in the Garret.

Handel's father was a doctor. He did not like music and would not let his children have music lessons.

But little George Frederick loved music so much that he could not do without it. So, somehow or other, he contrived to get either a clavichord or a small harpsichord into the garret, and there he taught himself to play. Or perhaps there was already an old clavichord or harpsichord among the lumber (in which case the little boy would surely have to tune it first, or get someone to do this for him).

He must have been about six years old when this happened.

There is a well-known picture which shows young George practising—and being caught in the act by his parents. History does not say whether he got a whipping, but if he did he cannot have minded it much, for he was far too determined to become a musician!

How he ran after the Coach.

The doctor had an elder son who was servant to a great Duke, about forty miles away. One day the father set off on a visit to him.

Now the Duke had music in his palace, so George wanted to go too, to hear it. The father would not consent to take him. When the coach had gone some distance the father heard a voice calling, and looking out he saw little George Frederick running behind. It was now too late to turn back and take him home, so he was allowed to go after all.

How he played to the Duke.

George soon made friends with the Duke's musicians, and they were kind to him because they felt he was one of themselves.

One day, after service in the Chapel of the Palace, the Duke was going out when he heard the organ played in a way that surprised him. He stopped and asked who was playing, and they told him it was the little boy who was staying in the Palace. The musicians had put him on the organ stool to see what the Duke would think of his music.

The Duke was so pleased with George's playing that he told his father it would be a sin to make the boy a lawyer, as he had thought of doing, and made him promise to give him a good musical education.

How he learnt Music.

In Halle, the town in Saxony where the Handel family lived, there was a good musician called Zachau. He was organist of the Cathedral, and had a head stuffed full with every sort of musical knowledge—how to compose in various different forms, and how to play the harpsichord and the organ and the violin and the hautboy. Handel's father thought this would be the very man to make a good musician of his son. So it was agreed that Zachau should give George music lessons.

For three years the lessons went on, and every week George wrote for his master a MOTET (a sort of anthem). Everybody in Halle thought him wonderful, and so he was. He had great talent not only for composing on paper but also for IMPROVISING (that is, playing the organ or harpsichord and making up the music as he went along).

After a time Zachau said, 'I cannot teach that boy anything more', so George's father sent him to Berlin.

Soon, however, the father died, and then George had to come back and begin to earn his living. When he was

seventeen the people at one of the chief churches were glad
to make so clever a youth their organist. He began to study at
the University at the same time.

How he began to earn his Living.

When Handel was eighteen he went to try his fortune in a
larger place—Hamburg. There was an opera house there,
and he became one of the violinists in the orchestra. Sometimes, too, when the conductor was away, he would take his
place, sitting at the harpsichord and playing it to keep the
band and singers together. (That was how conducting was
done in those times. Nowadays we use a stick or 'baton',
for the same purpose.)

Whilst at Hamburg, Handel wrote some operas which were
very much liked.

A Visit to Italy.

When Handel was twenty-one he decided to go to Italy,
which was then a great country for music. In many of the
cities they gave him a warm welcome, and he astonished the
Italians both by his playing and by his composing.

Handel learnt a great deal from the Italians, for they have
always been noted for two things—for writing effectively for
the *voice*, and for making beautiful *tunes*.

Handel in London.

From Italy Handel went home again to see his mother.
Whilst in Germany he had a great honour; the Elector of
Hanover made him his CAPELLMEISTER. (An Elector is a sort
of King on a small scale, and a Capellmeister a sort of
Conductor and Choirmaster on a large one.)

But Handel wanted to go to England, so the Elector gave
him leave to do so.

When he arrived in London he wrote a fine opera called
Rinaldo. This made a great stir, and he became famous. In

Rinaldo there is a garden scene, and to make it look real they had live sparrows and let them fly about.

All the well-to-do people of London went to see *Rinaldo*, and they treated Handel so well that after going home for a time, to his duties in Hanover, he soon came back again.

How he quarrelled with a King.

The second time Handel came to London he stayed quite a long time, and the Elector was very cross at his Capell-meister's absence. Then, suddenly, the Elector was called to England himself. In the history books we now call him not Elector of Hanover, but George I of England.

This was serious for Handel, for it is not a happy thing to be in bad favour with the king of the country in which you live. However, in time, the quarrel was made up.

The Water Music.

Later some friends of Handel had a good idea. The Royal Family were going down the river in a barge, and it was arranged that as they came back there should be another barge behind, with a band of musicians. It was agreed that Handel should write the music, and the King was very pleased with it. Handel was by now in high favour again, and the King gave him £200 a year for life, in addition to the pension Queen Anne had given him.

The music composed for the River Party just mentioned is called the *Water Music*.

Handel's Operas.

Rich people in London in those days were very fond of Operas, and Handel wrote a great many of them. Some people thought another composer, an Italian called Buononcini, wrote better operas than Handel, and soon there were two parties in London, supporting the one composer and running down the other. The King was, of course, on Handel's side, but the Prince of Wales was against him.

It was a pity that people quarrelled so, because it led to some of them starting a new opera house, and then each of the opera houses spent so much money in trying to get better singers and scenery than the other that both failed. So, when Handel was fifty-two, in spite of all his famous doings, he became almost bankrupt.

Handel's Oratorios.

It was really a good thing for the world that Handel failed in his opera work, because it made him try another plan— writing ORATORIOS. He said, 'I think, after all, sacred music is best suited for a man descending in the vale of years.'

That was how he came to write *Saul* (from which the great 'Dead March' comes), and *Judas Maccabaeus* (which is all about fighting), and *Israel in Egypt* (which is famous for its wonderful 'double choruses'—that is, choruses for two choirs singing at one time), and, greatest of all, *Messiah* (which is still often performed—at Christmas time especially). All these are Oratorios, that is, settings of sacred stories for solo singers and chorus and orchestra—in general style very much the same thing as Operas, except that they were merely to be sung and played, not acted.

How Handel went Blind and Died.

When Handel was about sixty he began to be ill. He went to Cheltenham to try if the waters would cure him, but he got slowly worse. Then, some years later, his eyesight failed (perhaps because he had done so much writing of music all his life). He had an operation for his eyesight, but it was no use, and in the last years he was quite blind.

He went bravely on, playing and conducting his music as usual, but one day, after conducting *Messiah*, he became dizzy and faint. That was the beginning of his last illness, and on Saturday morning, 14 April 1759, he passed away, aged seventy-four.

QUESTIONS

(TO SEE WHETHER YOU REMEMBER THE CHAPTER AND UNDERSTAND IT)

1. When was Handel born, and when did he die?

2. Tell any story that shows that he was very fond of music when a very small boy.

3. Did his father approve of his music? Tell any story showing how it came about that his father allowed him to have music lessons.

4. Who was the music teacher, and what did he learn?

5. What does 'Improvising' (or 'Improvisation') mean?

6. What is a Motet?

7. In what way did Handel begin to earn his living?

8. Why did Handel want to go to Italy? Did he learn anything there? Were the Italians kind to him?

9. What is a Capellmeister? To whom was Handel Capellmeister?

10. What did Handel do in London when he first went there? Mention an Opera he composed there.

11. How did Handel get into disgrace with George I?

12. What is an Oratorio?

13. How did Handel come to compose Oratorios?

14. Mention four of Handel's Oratorios.

15. What is a Double Chorus? Which Oratorio is famous for its Double Choruses?

16. What do you know about the ending of Handel's life?

THINGS TO DO

1. In some hymn-books you can find a hymn tune by Handel, which he wrote for the Methodists. It is called *Gopsal*, and its proper hymn (for which it was written)

is *Rejoice, the Lord is King*. Play it and see what it is like.

2. Handel's *Water Music* can be got arranged for piano, and also arranged for School Orchestra. Try to get it or hear it, and find out how each piece is made.

3. Try to get somebody to sing you a solo from *Messiah*.

4. If you have a Singing Class or School Choir, get your teacher to give you some solo or duet of Handel to practise as a choral piece. A good duet which will serve as a two-part chorus is *O Lovely Peace*. It is published in a form suitable for school choirs. After practising a piece like this look at the copy carefully and see how the piece is made. For instance, is it in Binary Form or Ternary Form—that is, is it a two-bit piece or a three-bit piece?

5. Play, or get somebody to play for you, the music of the Shepherds (the 'Pastoral Symphony') in *Messiah*. Listen to this carefully and discover as much as you can about the way it is made up. It is said that in this piece Handel recalls his experiences in Rome, when he was there as a young man and the shepherds used to come into the city to play their bagpipes for money at Christmas time. Do you hear anything in the piece that reminds you of bagpipes?

6. Handel wrote a good many Suites for Harpsichord that make jolly music for piano to-day. The little pieces which are strung together to make a Suite of Handel are generally some of the following:

Prelude, an opening piece.

Allemande, a fairly serious kind of piece with four beats in a bar, in the style of a dance called Allemande, which was perhaps (as the name indicates) of German origin.

Courante, a bright, running sort of piece ('courant' is, as you know, French for 'running'), with three beats in the bar, imitating a lively dance of the name 'Courante'.

Sarabande, a rather solemn sort of piece, with three very slow beats in the bar, imitating a stately Spanish dance of the same name.

Gigue, a piece in the style of a very lively dance, generally in what we call a 'compound time'—that is, with each beat divided into three smaller beats.

If you will look at these forms again you will see that after the Prelude comes a serious piece, followed by a lighter piece, followed by another serious piece, followed again by a lighter piece. So we get *variety*. Sometimes Handel gives the pieces in his Suites other names, but you always find this variety. Get somebody to play you a piece of each sort mentioned above and notice whether it corresponds in character with what you have just been told.

7. Now get somebody to play various pieces of Handel, several times each, whilst you listen carefully and find out how they are made up. Generally you will find there is a Cadence in the middle, as well as at the end, so that the piece falls into two parts—that is, it is in Binary Form. If you understand KEYS, notice in what key the beginning and end of the piece are, and in what key the middle Cadence. Often you will find that the whole piece is made out of one, two, or three tiny musical ideas used over and over again, sometimes high and sometimes low, sometimes in the right hand and sometimes in the left. Listen keenly, as the piece is played over and over again, until you feel you have found out all there is in it. This is the way to 'train your ears', so as to become a good listener.

8. A very jolly piece indeed is the Air and Variations in the 5th Suite (this Air and Variations is often called *The Harmonious Blacksmith*, but Handel never gave it that name and there is no blacksmith about it). Play this (it is not very difficult) or get somebody else to play it. First have the Air played several times, so as to get it well into your head, and

then have each Variation played several times to find out what Handel has done in each. Then have the whole set played straight through just for the fun of it.

This is the most popular of all Handel's Harpsichord pieces. Everybody loves it. But other pieces are just as fine, when you come to know them. Never be discouraged if you do not like a piece at first: there have been schoolfellows you did not care for at first, and afterwards, when you really knew them, they became your best friends.

9. Write and act a little play on some incident in Handel's life, bringing the performance of some of his music into it. There was a man who sold coals in London and held daily concerts at which Handel sometimes performed. Your teacher might look him up in *The Oxford Companion to Music*, Grove's *Dictionary of Music*, or in the *Dictionary of National Biography*, and then tell you enough about him for you to give a little play called *The Coalman's Concert*. (His name was Thomas Britton.)

10. Look out for any Handel music in the broadcast programmes and in *The Radio Times*, and when you find any, make a note of the day and time, so as not to miss it.

11. When buying Gramophone Records, ask the dealer what Handel records he has got, or can get for you.

V

JOHN SEBASTIAN BACH
1685–1750

The Merry Miller and his Descendants.

There was once in Germany a merry miller, whose name was Veit Bach. Besides being a miller he was also a musician and whilst his mill was grinding away he would twang his zither, and, we may imagine, troll out a jolly song

Now Veit had a son named Hans, who was a carpet weaver by trade, but, like his jovial old father, a musician as well. He played the violin, so, perhaps, the father and son played duets sometimes, for a zither and a violin would go pretty well together.

Hans, too, had a son, and he was called Christopher. He became chief musician to a great nobleman and had two boys, twins. They looked just alike, and, funnily enough, he called them both by the same first name, John—so they must have been very confusing when they were at school, especially if they were dressed alike. Their second names, however, were different. One was John Christopher, and the other John Ambrose. They were both good performers on the fiddle and played other instruments as well.

In his turn John Ambrose had two sons, and they were both great organ players and composers, but the younger was the cleverer, and he was called JOHN SEBASTIAN BACH. All this is told here in order to show you what a musical family the Bachs were.

The Orphan.

When John Sebastian was only ten years old, his father and mother died, and he had to go to live with his elder brother.

He could already play the violin, for his father had taught him to do that.

The brother sent him to school, to learn his ordinary lessons, and himself taught him to play the clavichord and harpsichord. But the boy could soon play all his music by heart, and then he wanted something more difficult.

Now the brother had a book of music of which he was very proud. It was all written by hand and had in it beautiful pieces by all the great composers of those days.

He never let little Sebastian play from this book. Perhaps he was jealous of him, and feared he would learn to play better than himself; or, perhaps, the little boy sometimes had dirty or sticky fingers, as boys in those days sometimes had.

At any rate John Christopher kept this wonderful book carefully locked up in a cupboard. But John Sebastian made up his mind to learn the pieces in the book, so he managed to roll it up and pull it through the latticed door of the cupboard. At night he would do this, and then, by moonlight, set to work to copy all the beautiful pieces into a book of his own.

One night, however, his brother caught him, and then all his work was largely wasted, for his copy of the book was taken from him. It had taken six months to make. Still the labour was not altogether thrown away, for we may be sure that the copying had taught him a good deal about music and how it is composed.

Holiday Tramps.

Soon after this, Bach went to school at a place called Luneberg. There were good organists to be heard there, and he used to learn a good deal by listening to them. But at Hamburg, miles away, was a greater organist still, a famous old Dutchman, called Reinken.

When holidays came round, Bach used to put some food in his pocket, and all the money he had been able to save, and trudge off to hear the great organist.

One day he had been on one of these expeditions and was tramping back. His money was nearly spent, and when he came to an inn he did not dare go inside, but sat outside smelling the delicious things that were being cooked and wishing he could buy some of them.

Suddenly the window opened, and out at his feet fell two herrings' heads. He picked them up and inside each of them he found a silver coin. So he was able not only to satisfy his hunger, but actually to turn back again to Hamburg, to hear some more of the wonderful music.

Who was it who threw the money? He never found out, and now we shall never know.

The Young Organist.

When he was eighteen years old, Bach became a violinist in the band of a Prince. After a few months, however, he left this band to become organist of a church at Armstadt.

He soon got into trouble at the church where he played, because he went to Lübeck to hear the music there under the famous Danish organist, Buxtehude, and became so wrapped up in it that he stayed three months.

When he came back they found fault with him not only for his absence, but also because, when he accompanied the CHORALES (or hymn tunes) on the organ, he put such wonderful accompaniments to them that he disturbed the people in their singing.

His fame as an organist was, however, very great, and during the next few years, in his several organist's posts, he became recognized as the best organ player of the day.

He wrote most of his famous organ pieces at this time of his life.

The Prince's Chamber Music.

When Bach was thirty-two he took service with a Prince, at Cöthen, as his Capellmeister. Here he did not have to play the organ, but to direct the chamber music for the court concerts. So this was a time when he composed no church music, but, instead of that, a great deal of beautiful music for other instruments than the organ.

The Prince loved music, and was so fond of Bach that he made him go with him on his long journeys.

Bach at Leipzig.

When Bach was thirty-eight he made the last move of his life—to Leipzig. Here he was 'Cantor' at the Thomas School and Director of the Music in two churches. He had to teach singing and to give the younger boys in the school lessons in Latin. At the University he conducted the students' musical society. It was a very important position that he held.

A House of Music.

Bach's house at Leipzig was overflowing with music. His wife sang and all his children were clever musicians. Then, too, he had a lot of pupils about the house. They came from far and near to learn from him.

Whenever any musicians came to Leipzig they always went to Bach's house to pay their respects to him.

Just as he wrote organ music in his earlier life (when he was mainly an organist), and other instrumental music in his middle life (when he was chief chamber musician to the Prince), so he now wrote beautiful church music such as Motets and Cantatas and Passion Music for the two churches with which he was connected. A CANTATA is something like a short Oratorio. PASSION MUSIC is also like an Oratorio and tells the story of the last days of Christ.

The King sends for Bach.

When Bach was sixty-one years old he got an invitation from Frederick the Great to come to his court at Berlin. One of Bach's sons was a musician at this court, and Bach was no doubt glad to have a chance of seeing him, as well as honoured by the King's request.

As soon as he got to the court, they told the King, who was playing the flute, but who put it down and announced to his courtiers: 'Gentlemen, old Bach is come!' He made him play, just as he was, and without giving him time to remove the dust of travel.

Whilst Bach was at the court, the King made him improvise a great deal, and also try all his organs and pianos. The piano was still a new instrument, and Bach preferred the harpsichord, or, still more, the clavichord.

Keyboard Instruments.

Pianoforte, Harpsichord, Clavichord, and Organ all have keyboards, but

1. The Pianoforte has Hammers to strike the strings.

2. The Harpsichord has Quills to pluck them.[1]

3. The Clavichord has what are called 'Tangents', which cut off (as it were) the right length of string to make the note, and strike it at the same time.

4. The Organ has pipes, not strings.

Bach goes Blind.

Like Handel, Bach went blind in old age. All his life he had been so busy copying and playing music that he had strained his eyes.

Bach died at Leipzig in 1750, aged sixty-five years. He is often spoken of as the greatest musician who ever lived.

[1] The Virginals was a small Harpsichord.

QUESTIONS

(TO SEE WHETHER YOU REMEMBER THE CHAPTER
AND UNDERSTAND IT)

1. Handel belonged to an unmusical family. Did Bach? Tell anything you happen to remember about his father, uncle, grandfather, and great-grandfather.

2. What do you know about Bach's early life in his brother's house?

3. What was Bach's first post? And what was his next?

4. What is a Chorale? How did Bach's playing of the Chorales get him into trouble when he was a young man?

5. What were Bach's duties in his next important post?

6. What was his last post, and how long did he occupy it? (You can easily reckon.)

7. What sort of music did Bach write in his last post?

8. What is a Cantata? What is Passion Music?

9. Tell the story of the meeting of Frederick the Great and Bach.

10. What are the four keyboard instruments, and how is the sound produced in each?

11. What do you know of Bach's last years?

THINGS TO DO

1. Most hymn-tune books have some Chorales composed by Bach or else older ones *harmonized* by him (that is, the tune, or treble part, was old, but Bach wrote the alto, tenor, and bass parts to it). Look through a hymn-book for these and play them, so as to get a good idea of what a Chorale is like. Bach made a great deal of use of Chorales in his Cantatas and Passion Music.

2. If you can, get hold of a copy of Bach's *Christmas Oratorio*, and get somebody to play the Pastoral Symphony

out of that (the piece that begins Part II) and compare it with Handel's Pastoral Symphony in *Messiah.*

3. Now get somebody to play you a Suite of Bach's, just as they did a Suite of Handel's, so that you can compare the two styles. Notice again the *variety* in the pieces.

Then as in the case of Handel, have an Allemande played separately and study how it is made, and do the same with a Courante, a Sarabande, and a Gigue—or several of each.

4. Besides the Allemande, Courante, Sarabande, and Gigue, Bach almost always adds some more pieces (generally just before the Gigue); some of these are as follows:

Bourrée, a lively old French dance with four beats in a bar, and every phrase beginning on the fourth beat of the bar.[1]

Gavotte, like the Bourrée, but with every phrase beginning on the third beat of a bar.

Menuet (or Minuet), a fairly stately, yet bright, dance with three beats in a bar.

Get somebody to play you one of each of these from Bach's Suites, and so get to know their style. Then have each played several times and study carefully how it is made up.

5. If possible, get somebody to play you a Violin piece of Bach, and then study how that is made. Always after studying a piece carefully have it played once more, just for fun.

6. Make up a little play on some incident in Bach's life, bringing in a performance of some of his music.

7. Look out for any Bach music in the broadcast programmes and in *The Radio Times*, and when you find any, make a note of the day and time, so as not to miss it.

8. When buying Gramophone Records, ask the dealer what Bach records he has got, or can get for you.

[1] Music is divided into 'phrases' which are something like separate lines of a piece of poetry. In the folk-songs on pages 3 and 4 you will see the phrases shown by the 'slurs', or curved lines, placed over the notes.

VI

'C–O–N–T–R–A–P–U–N–T–A–L'

A BIG WORD EXPLAINED

I

THERE is a big, long, ugly word which is often used to describe such music as that of Bach and Handel. The word is C–O–N–T–R–A–P–U–N–T–A–L. Let us understand it.

2

You know there is (or used to be) a form of government called **Absolute Monarchy**. In countries that have this, one man governs and has his own way, and the rest just support him and do as they are told.

3

Then there is the very opposite form of government called a Republic. Here all are supposed to take their share of the management of the country. As the Irishman said of America, 'Every man is as good as every other man, and sometimes better.'

4

Now music also falls into two classes. In one class there is a beautiful tune in the top part, and all the other parts underneath simply support it with harmony.

Play the *Old Hundredth*, or almost any hymn tune, and you will find this to be the case. First play the top part (the tune) and then play in turn the Alto, Tenor, and Bass parts. You will find these underneath parts have little interest in themselves.

Now play the whole thing, with all its four parts, and you will find that the under parts, whilst (as we found) not of great interest in themselves, serve to support the top part and make it more interesting. We say that such a piece has a MELODY or tune (at the top) and that it has HARMONY (or chords) to support the tune. That is 'Absolute Monarchy' in Music.

5

Now play just a few lines from a chorus of Handel's *Messiah*. You will generally find that every voice has a tune of its own, or else imitates the tune of one of the others. So here there is MELODY, and HARMONY too (for all the voices combine together to make chords). But in addition there is COUNTERPOINT (that is, tune in every part).

6

Nearly all the music you have so far heard as illustrations of this book has been Contrapuntal.

You remember the Catches in Chapter II. Those, of course, were Contrapuntal, because every voice that was singing had a real tune—the same tune, as it happened, in this case.

Then, the Elizabethan hymn tune on page 13 was Contrapuntal, for the Tenor had a real tune, which, in this case was the same as that of the Treble (the Alto and Bass parts were not very 'tuney' in this piece; try them over and you will find that they do little more than fill up the Harmony).

Nearly all the Keyboard Music of the Elizabethan composers and of Purcell and Bach and Handel was more or less Contrapuntal, and some of it was entirely so, that is, although meant to be played by fingers it was written in 'parts' or 'voices' almost as if intended to be sung, and each of the 'parts' or 'voices' had real tune in it. Some of the pieces, it is true, had passages in them that were merely 'harmonic', but, in that case, there soon came back again passages with Counterpoint in them.

A piece of 'contrapuntal' music is like a piece of beautiful tapestry. A number of threads are woven together to make the fabric. Each thread is beautiful in itself, and combined they make a beautiful whole.

7

So now you know what is meant by saying 'The music of Bach and Handel is Contrapuntal'.

QUESTIONS

(TO SEE WHETHER YOU REMEMBER THE CHAPTER
AND UNDERSTAND IT)

1. If we say that a piece has a good 'Melody', what do we mean?

2. If we say it has good 'Harmony', what do we mean?

3. If we say it is 'in good Counterpoint', what do we mean?

SOMETHING TO DO

Most people can easily appreciate a piece with one good Melody, at the top.

And most people can also appreciate good Harmony. But if there is Counterpoint they very often lose it altogether, because their ears are not trained to hear two or three melodies going on at the same time. They can generally hear the top part (or 'voice'), but they miss the lower part or parts.

There is a game you can play, which will train you to hear lower parts. It takes two to play it, but more can join.

We will suppose two are playing it. Each of them prepares at home six puzzles made like the following, with a well-known tune below and another specially made-up tune written above to disguise it. Each player then, in turn, plays one of his tunes (with its disguise, of course) and the other has to find out what it is. If he finds out the very first time the tune is played it counts 1; if he finds out the second time it is played it counts 2; if the third time it counts 3—and so on down to 6, if he finds out the sixth time it is played. If he cannot find out the tune in six 'goes' it counts ten. The one who gets the smaller number of marks wins, of course. The game is called

'CAMOUFLAGED TUNES'

Well known to everybody—

Well known to Scotsmen—

Often heard in Church—

Another Church tune—

A Northern Song—

A Convivial Song—

(Top part to be played *staccato*.)

Before you look at the above tunes get somebody to play them carefully to you, and see how few marks you can get. Listen *hard* to the lower 'voice'.

You may think this a difficult game to play, because the 'camouflage' has to be made up before you begin. But it is in the rules of the game that you can use the piano to help you to find a camouflage. What you do first, of course, is to write down the tune itself, and you then try to find notes that will go with it to make a good camouflage. Most people can soon learn how to do this even if they have never had lessons in Harmony and Counterpoint.

Of course if you have not learnt to write music you cannot play this game, but in that case perhaps you can get your teacher to make up some 'Camouflages' and to play the game with the class.

Do not be discouraged if you find this game harder to play than you expected. Some people find it very hard to hear an underneath part until they get the 'knack' of it; others find it easy.

One way of making the game a little easier is to have the tune played an octave lower (leaving the camouflage in its old place). If the game is *still* too hard, make it a rule that this tune shall be played a little louder than the 'camouflage'.

VII

ALL ABOUT FUGUES AND HOW TO LISTEN TO THEM

BACH and Handel wrote many pieces which are called FUGUES. Some of these anybody can appreciate right away, because they have a jolly swing about them. But others are not so easy to understand, and so some people, feeling rather bewildered, make up their minds that to appreciate a Fugue is beyond *them*, and give up trying. But if you know how Fugues are made it is not, as a matter of fact, very hard to understand them, and once you do understand a good Fugue you get fonder and fonder of it, until, at last, hearing that Fugue (or playing it) becomes one of the great pleasures of your life. It is worth a little study and effort to add a new pleasure to life, and this is why this chapter is written.

Fugues are in 'Voices'.

The first thing to tell you about a Fugue is that it is entirely (or almost entirely) 'Contrapuntal'. It may be a Fugue for keyboard, yet at the beginning you will generally see the words 'In three voices', or 'In four voices', or 'In five voices', and so you see, although there may be no *real* voices it is written and performed as though it were actually to be sung by three or four or five people, or sets of people in a choir.

Of course some Fugues are meant really to be sung. Handel's *Messiah*, for instance, has Fugues for choir.

A Fugue has a 'Subject'.

A Fugue is largely made out of a little bit of tune which we call its 'subject'. The Subject of a Fugue is generally like the text of a sermon—nearly the whole thing is supposed to be made out of it.

Here are one or two of Bach's Fugue Subjects, which will give you an idea of what such things are like.

A rather gay Subject in the minor—

A quiet, happy Subject in the major—

A fairly solemn Subject—

A really quite skittish and rather long Subject—

(Play these Subjects neatly and rhythmically, or get some-body to play them to you.)

How the Fugue begins.

The Fugue begins by one of the 'voices' giving out the Subject; then, whilst this 'voice' goes on with something else, another comes in with the Subject, so that now two 'voices' are getting on together—one with the Subject, and one with 'something else'. Then a third voice comes in with the Subject, whilst the other two go on with 'something else',

so that three are going on together—and so on until all
the voices have had their turn. You will see that this
part of a Fugue is something like the Rounds you sang in
Chapter II.

But there is one special thing you must be told about these
voices and the Subject. The first voice brings in the Subject
in the proper chief key of the piece, the second one brings it
in in the key of five notes higher (or four notes lower),[1] the
third brings it in in the old key again, and so on.

The entries of the Subject that are in the '*other* key' we call
ANSWER. We can make diagrams of this part of the Fugue
(which we call its EXPOSITION) if you like. Here is a diagram
of a Fugue in five 'voices' in Key C.

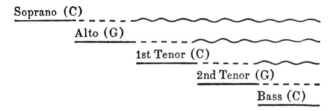

In this Fugue, as you see, the top voice came in first.

Now we will have a Fugue in Key E, with one of the
middle voices beginning.

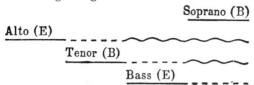

So that is all clear and easy to understand, is it not? And
now the thing is to get somebody to play you the 'Exposi-
tions' of three or four Fugues, so that you can learn to listen
for the Subject coming in in each voice in turn.

[1] This we call the 'Dominant' Key (i.e. the note that was 'Dominant' or
Soh is now the new 'Tonic' or *Doh*).

Sometimes the voice that has just sung the Subject (or Answer) goes on with another Subject, which we call a COUNTER-SUBJECT. The Subject and Counter-Subject together are, as you will no doubt realize, something like one of the tunes on page 43 with its 'Camouflage'. In the diagrams above, the Subject is shown by a straight line, the Counter-Subject by a dotted line, and everything else by wavy lines. Look carefully again at those diagrams, please, and get them fixed in your mind's eye so firmly that they will always stay there.

Episodes—and then more 'Entries'.

You know what an 'episode' is in a story. The author leaves the main plot of the story for the moment, and goes on to tell you of a little incident that is not really part of the main plot, but still has something to do with it. A Fugue has episodes like that, and after the Exposition we usually have such an Episode. Generally you will find that this is made out of some little bit of the Subject or Counter-Subject, and it is interesting to listen keenly to the Episode and find out how it *is* made.

The first Episode takes us into some other key, and then the Subject comes in again, perhaps in one part, perhaps in two, or three, or all. We say that it 'enters' and call this an Entry.

Then follows a second Episode, and a further 'Entry' in still another key, and so on to the end of the Fugue, where the Subject comes back at last in its old key—the main key of the piece.

'Stretto'.

Sometimes in one or more of the Entries the Subject comes in in several voices, one voice entering with the Subject before the other has finished with it. This we call a STRETTO. If we made a diagram of it, it would look like this

Soprano ‿‿‿‿‿‿‿‿‿

Alto ‿‿‿‿‿‿‿

Tenor ‿‿‿‿‿‿‿

That, as you will see, is *very much* like a Catch or a Canon. The Subject 'overlaps'. The voices come in with it one after the other, treading on one another's tails.

Pedal.

Sometimes, in an Organ piece, as you may have noticed, the player puts his foot on one of the low notes which are played by pedals, and keeps it held down and booming away whilst with his hands he plays the upper 'voices' of his music. This is also done in Piano Fugues (only here, of course, it is done with the little finger of the left hand), and it is also done in Choral Fugues (only here the low note is sung by the basses). But we always call such a note a PEDAL, whether it is on the Organ or on the Piano, or sung by a Choir, or played by the bass instruments in an Orchestra. The effect is generally rather thrilling.

Preludes.

Many of Bach's Fugues have a piece before them which we call a PRELUDE. Bach wrote two big books of Preludes and Fugues, each with a Prelude and Fugue in every major key (twelve, that is) and in every minor key (another twelve). Each book has thus twenty-four Preludes and Fugues, making in all what we often call 'Bach's 48', or sometimes his *Well-tempered Clavier*.[1]

[1] 'Well-tempered' means tuned in the modern way instead of in a certain old-fashioned way, which only allowed you to play in a few particular keys because it sounded harsh in all the others. Clavier means a keyboard or keyboard instrument (Clavichord, Harpsichord—or to-day, Pianoforte).

E I

QUESTIONS

(TO SEE WHETHER YOU REMEMBER THE CHAPTER
AND UNDERSTAND IT)

1. What do we mean when we say 'That Fugue is in four voices'?
2. What is the 'Subject' of a Fugue?
3. What is the 'Answer'?
4. What is a 'Counter-Subject'?
5. Describe the 'Exposition' of a Fugue.
6. Without looking at p. 47 make a diagram of an Exposition of an imaginary Fugue in four voices, with the Subject coming first in the bass.
7. Now do another one, in three voices, with the Subject coming first in the middle voice.
8. What is an 'Episode'?
9. What is an 'Entry'?
10. What is a 'Stretto'?
11. What is a 'Pedal'?
12. What is 'Bach's 48'? What is its other name?

(If you can answer all those questions correctly you know a great deal about Fugues—far more than many grown-up musical people. Yet, you see, it is not really a difficult matter.)

THINGS TO DO

1. If you play the Piano, and are advanced enough to play a Fugue, get your teacher to give you one and then mark in pencil the Subject, Answer, Counter-Subject (if there is one), Episodes, and all the other features.

Then practise it carefully and play it to somebody, first playing all the different features separately and explaining them, and then playing the whole Fugue several times to see if they understand it. Then you will really be giving a little Lecture on 'How to understand a Fugue'.

2. Get your Teacher or some pianist friend to play Fugues to you, seeing how much you can find out about them just by ear and without looking at the music. Can you answer these questions after hearing it twice or three times?

(a) How many voices has this Fugue?
(b) How many Entries has it after the Exposition?
(c) Has it any Stretto?
(d) Has it a Pedal?

3. If you know an organist ask him to play you a good Fugue on the organ. Tell him you prefer a merry one, if he has such a thing, but, if not, a solemn one will do. An organist often plays Fugues after the service, but generally the people are in such a hurry to get out that they only hear a bit of the Exposition.

4. If *Messiah* is going to be performed, go to hear it, but, before you go, get some good pianist to play you some of the choruses, and study how they are made. Also study the Fugue which forms part of the Overture.

5. Try to get a gramophone record of a Fugue and then listen to it, over and over again, finding out all about it by very careful listening. (You can get the *Messiah* Overture as a record, for one.)

VIII

HAYDN

1732–1809

A Musical Family.

Haydn was born in a place called Rohrau, in Austria. As his father was only a village wheelwright, there can hardly have been much money to spare for luxury. Nevertheless the family was a very happy one, and a great pleasure they had was plenty of music. The father had a tenor voice, and accompanied his own singing on the harp, two of the brothers must have been musical, for they became professional musicians when they grew up, and Joseph himself had a beautiful voice, and, besides, used to sit on the bench by the fire and pretend to play the violin like the village schoolmaster, but with two pieces of stick for the instrument and bow.

How Haydn went to the Town.

One day, whilst little Joseph was singing and pretending to play, there came in a relative, a musician in the town near by. He thought the little boy must have music in him, and so begged the parents to let him take him away to be trained.

So Haydn became a choir-boy, and worked hard to make himself a good musician. He got 'more flogging than food', he used to say in after-life, when he looked back, but yet he felt grateful to his relative. 'Almighty God', he said, 'to whom I render thanks for all his unnumbered mercies, gave me such facility in music, that by the time I was six, I stood up like a man and sang masses in the church choir, and could play a little on the harpsichord and violin.'

A Cathedral Choir-boy.

There came to the town one day an important man—choir-master of the great St. Stephen's Cathedral in Vienna. He heard Haydn sing, and, after putting him through an examination to see what he knew, he said he would take him to be a choir-boy in the Cathedral. So to Vienna little eight-year-old Joseph went. Here he learnt singing and harpsichord and violin playing from good masters.

What troubled Haydn was that they did not teach him to compose. He wanted to write music as well as to sing it and play it. However, as they did not teach him, he thought he would teach himself, so he got every piece of music-paper he could find, and covered it with notes. 'It must be all right if the paper is nice and full,' he said. One day the Cathedral choirmaster found him trying to write a great piece of church music in twelve voices, and advised him to write in two first of all. But he never showed him how to do it, and the little boy had to struggle and find that out for himself.

By and by, Joseph's brother, Michael, became a chorister at the Cathedral, too. This was very nice for both of them, but at last Joseph's voice began to break, and then the choirmaster used to put his younger brother up to sing the solos before the Emperor and Empress, which was mortifying for poor Joseph.

Then the choirmaster began to want to get rid of Joseph, and waited for an opportunity. Now the choir-boys all had pigtails, and one day, Haydn, being in a mischievous mood, and having a new pair of scissors he wanted to try, snipped off the pigtail of one of the other boys. So the master gave him a good thrashing and turned him adrift.

The Hungry Haydn.

Many great men have gone through a time of hunger, and so did Haydn now. He had a big boyish appetite, and no money to buy food. However, friends helped him a little, and he hired an attic, and got hold of an old worm-eaten harpsichord. There he sat, day after day, playing and studying the Sonatas of Emanuel Bach (son of the great Sebastian), and then trying to write others like them. He also practised the violin.

Fortunately, after a time he became known to a famous singing teacher called Porpora, and was invited to act as accompanist at the singing lessons. In this way he learned a great deal about the voice, and also met many famous musicians, who gave him advice—for Porpora knew them all.

All this time, and all his life, Haydn was a very hard worker, and that is one reason why he became so great.

Haydn becomes 'Capellmeister'.

Gradually Haydn's musicianship became known, and at last a great chance came to him, for a Count Morzin made him his chief musician. In return for his labours he had his board and lodging, and twenty pounds a year. This he thought was wealth, so he straightway got married.

The Count sometimes had a famous visitor, Prince Anton Esterhazy. By and by, when Count Morzin decided to give up his band, Prince Esterhazy engaged Haydn, and then he had to direct an orchestra and chorus, church music, concerts, and operas. That was a splendid thing for Haydn, because it gave him such an opportunity of gaining experience, and when he wrote a piece of music he could have it tried, see what it sounded like, and then sit down and write a better one. The time was largely spent on the Prince's country estate, and Haydn said, in after life: 'I was cut off from the world, there was no one to confuse or torment me, and I was forced to become original.'

Haydn in England.

English musical people had heard a great deal about Haydn, and had pressed him to come to England, but he could not do so. At last the Prince died and he was free. A London conductor, named Salomon, was in Germany when this occurred, and he at once set off to see Haydn. He persuaded him to come to London, and they started together. This was in 1790, when Haydn was fifty-eight years of age. It was on New Year's Day that Salomon and Haydn crossed from Calais to Dover. There were no steamboats then and it took nine hours.

When they got to London everybody flocked to welcome Haydn, and the University of Oxford invited him to go up to receive the degree of Mus.Doc. The Prince of Wales became a great friend of his, and used to play the violoncello whilst he played the harpsichord.

Haydn stayed in England eighteen months, and after some time in Austria came back again in 1798. He wrote some splendid Symphonies for London Concerts. One of these he called the 'Surprise Symphony', because, in one movement, he lulls the audience almost to sleep by his quiet music, and then suddenly wakes them up with a loud chord.

The Last Concert.

When Haydn was an old man of seventy-six they carried him in his arm-chair to hear a performance of his great Oratorio *The Creation*. They placed him there in the centre of the hall, amongst the greatest people of the land, and clapped and cheered until they were tired. Then the performance began and Haydn became very excited. When the concert was half over they thought it best to take him home, and as he went out at the door a famous musician of about forty years of age kissed him. This was his former pupil, Beethoven.

Haydn then turned round and held up his hands, as if blessing the people, and for the last time looked on an audience gathered to hear his music. This was his last public appearance, and shortly after it he died.

QUESTIONS

1. Was Haydn a Frenchman or an Italian or a German—or what was he?

2. Had he a long life or a short one? When was he born and when did he die?

3. What do you remember about his family?

4. What age was he when he began to earn his living by music?

5. Why was he turned out of his place? And what did he then do?

6. Think over all you have just read about his early life, and then say what you remember about his musical education. What did he learn, and how?

7. When Haydn obtained his important post as Capell-meister to the Prince, what were his duties?

8. Tell anything you remember about Haydn in England.

9. What Oratorio did Haydn write?

THINGS TO DO

1. Get somebody to play you music by Haydn, and listen carefully to find out how it is made up. They might play an air and variations from one of the Symphonies, or any slow movement from a Sonata or Symphony. Or they might play you or sing you something out of *The Creation*. (The longer movements of the Sonatas and Symphonies should be left until you have done Chapter X.) Besides finding out how the pieces are made, try to get an idea of Haydn's style, and the *flavour* of his music, so that if some day you hear somebody playing one of his pieces that you have never heard before you may be able to say, 'Oh, that must be a piece by Haydn!'

2. When Haydn was in England he admired the tune of 'God save the King'[1] so much that he decided to write a national anthem for his own country. So he wrote what is often called *Haydn's Hymn for the Emperor*, which will be found in almost any hymn-tune book under the name *Austria*.

3. Make up and act a little play on one of the incidents of Haydn's life.

4. If you can play the piano, get some of Haydn's music arranged for piano duet and play it with a friend.

5. If you like dancing, get a Haydn Minuet (perhaps from one of the Symphonies) and make up a dance to it.

6. If you have a school band, get some of Haydn's music for it.

7. And if you have a school choir, ask for some Haydn music for that.

8. Look out for any Haydn music in the broadcast programmes and in *The Radio Times*, and when you find any, make a note of the day and time, so as not to miss it.

9. When buying Gramophone Records, ask the dealer what Haydn records he has got, or can get for you.

[1] American children sing this tune, the British National Anthem, to *My country 'tis of thee*.

IX

MOZART

1756–1791

Two Children on Tour.

A little boy of six and his sister of eleven, with their father to take care of them, were making a concert tour. Both the children played the harpsichord beautifully, and some of the pieces they played were their own compositions. First they went to Munich, and played before the great Elector; then, as every one had praised their playing so much, they went to Vienna. On the way they had often to stop and give little performances to the rich and great people whose houses they passed, for their fame had gone before them.

When they came to a place called Ips, where there was a Franciscan monastery, the little boy sat down at the organ and played so well that the monks all left their dinner, and came into the choir to hear him.

In the Customs-House.

The children played the violin, as well as the harpsichord, and the father, writing home to the mother, told how music had been useful when they had to pass through the customs-house at Vienna. He said:

'Our business with the revenue officers was short, and from the principal search we were entirely absolved. For this we had to thank Mr. Woferl, who made friends with the *douanier*, showed him his clavier, and played him a minuet on his little violin.'

'Mr. Woferl' was the pet name for the little boy, Wolfgang Amadeus Mozart; as for 'douanier', you all know French, of course, so there is no need to tell you that this means customs officer. 'Clavier' is a word that would do for any sort of keyboard instrument, but here it means a harpsichord (perhaps a small one, such as the little party would be easily able to take about with them).

How they appeared at Court.

It was a great day for the father when he got a summons from the Emperor to bring his children to court. Woferl was too little, however, to feel what an honour this was, and when they got there, he sprang into the lap of the Empress, clasped her round the neck, and kissed her very heartily.

How Woferl offered to marry a Princess.

Woferl was such a little boy that he could not be expected to behave like a courtier. He used to run and jump about the room, and once, when he fell on the slippery floor, the Princess Marie Antoinette helped him to get up, and he said to her: 'You are good, and I will marry you.'

The Princess was then a little girl, being only a year older than himself. As you know, she did *not* marry Mozart, but became Queen of France.

About thirty years after this little incident poor Marie Antoinette lost her life by the guillotine. When she was being tried her cruel accusers noticed that she sometimes moved her fingers as if playing the harpsichord. So we see that she was a musician too, and we can imagine that when she was going through that awful experience, she cheered herself by thinking she was playing some of her favourite pieces—quite possibly pieces by her old friend, Mozart.

In Court Dress.

The stay at Vienna was very jolly for the children. The Emperor made them valuable gifts, and paid the father well. Marianne had given to her a grand court dress of white silk, which had belonged to one of the young Archduchesses, and Wolfgang received a violet-coloured suit, trimmed with gold braid, which had been made for a little Archduke. The father was very proud of his children, and had their picture painted, dressed in this splendid fashion.

This enjoyable visit came to an end through the little boy catching scarlet fever, for when he recovered it was thought best to return to Salzburg.

Paris and London.

Next year, however, they all set off on their travels once more. This time they went to Paris, where they had a great welcome, and then to London. You will remember that there were no trains or steamers in those days, so that the travelling had to be done by coach and sailing boat. The boat to Dover made them all very sick, but they soon got over this, and went on to London to see the King.

How the Children played to George III.

The King was astonished at Wolfgang's playing. This is what the father wrote home to the mother at Salzburg:

'The King placed before him pieces by Wagenseil, Bach, Abel, and Handel, all of which he played off. He played on the King's organ in such a manner that his hearers preferred him on the organ to the clavier. He then accompanied the Queen in an air, and a performer on the flute in a solo. At last he took up the bass part of one of Handel's airs that by chance lay in the way, and, upon the mere bass, performed a melody so beautiful that it astonished everybody.'

How the Father fell ill in England.

Whilst they were in England the father fell dangerously ill. They were obliged to be as still as mice, so as not to disturb the invalid, and, as Wolfgang could not play, he composed.

He filled a manuscript book with his compositions, and this has lately been printed, and is very interesting indeed.

Mozart's first Symphony was written at this time. His sister sat by him as he wrote it, and he said: 'Remind me that I give the horns something good to do.'

When the father recovered the children gave many concerts, and the orchestra used to play the Symphonies that the young composer was now writing.

The Happy Boyhood ended.

And now we must pass on from those boyish days, and we shall be saddened to find that poor Mozart's happiness did not last. It really seems as though there are a great many people in the world who welcome a clever boy musician rather because he is a *boy* than for the sake of his *music*. When Mozart was a young man, he found that the great people who had treated him so kindly were no longer much interested in him. He went to Paris again, taking his mother with him. He had to take a poor little lodging, so small that there was no room even for a harpsichord. Wolfgang's old friend, Marie Antoinette, was now Queen of France, but he could not find any one who could take him to court and present him to her.

A Rude Duchess.

Some one gave him an introduction to a great society lady, the Duchess of Chabot, who invited him to call. But when he did so, he was first allowed to stay for half an hour in an ice-cold waiting-room, and then to sit for an hour whilst the Duchess sat at a table with some gentlemen, drawing.

Then they asked him to play the piano, but went on all the time with their occupation, and when they praised his playing he knew that they were only giving him worthless compliments.

But the greatest misfortune in Paris was the death of his

mother. After this he was quite alone in the great city, and very much he felt it.

Mozart and the Archbishop.

After all these troubles we may be sure the young man was glad to get back home to Salzburg. Here his father obtained for him the position of Court Organist to the Archbishop.

The Archbishop was proud, and whilst he was glad to have a great musician like young Mozart in his employment, he did not treat him with respect. At meals the Court Organist had to sit with the valets and cooks. The pay he received was very small and was not given him promptly. Then his master would very rarely give him permission to play anywhere but in his own house.

At last poor Mozart could stand this life no longer, so he sent in his resignation. The Archbishop used rough and rude language to him, and the High Steward was very violent, and it is even said that he kicked Mozart out of doors.

The Operas.

Happily, Mozart's luck was not always so bad as this, and it is pleasant to know that soon after he had left the Archbishop people began to realize what a wonderful composer of Operas they had in him. So Mozart had some very joyous experiences, as well as some sad ones, in his grown-up life.

Mozart's Operas number about twenty: the best known are *Figaro*, *The Magic Flute*, and *Don Giovanni*.

Mozart's Death.

It is sad to think that Mozart's last work was a REQUIEM, that is to say, a Mass for the Dead. He wrote this on his death-bed. When he died, his wife, who loved him dearly, was so overcome with grief that she could not go to the funeral, and when she was sufficiently recovered to visit the churchyard, nobody could tell her where her husband had been buried.

It seems a pitiful thing that this great man should have died at so early an age as thirty-five, and that the world should have taken so little interest in its loss of him that people did not even mark his grave.

QUESTIONS

(TO SEE WHETHER YOU REMEMBER THE CHAPTER
AND UNDERSTAND IT)

1. When was Mozart born and when did he die? How long was his life?

2. Tell all you remember about the childhood of Mozart and his sister. This should be quite a lot—experiences in Vienna, Paris, London, &c. If you are studying this Chapter in class with your friends, have a competition to see who can remember most.

3. Tell all you remember about his troubles when he became a young man.

4. What are the names of some of Mozart's most famous operas?

THINGS TO DO

1. If you play the piano, get your teacher to give you some music by Mozart. Some of the movements in the Sonatas are interesting, but others are now old-fashioned and sound soulless and thin: ask your teacher to give you the interesting pieces.

2. Get somebody to play you some of Mozart's shorter pieces and try to find how they are made up. In one of the Sonatas there is an Air with Variations that everybody likes, and there are also some Minuets that are quite jolly. (Keep

the long movements of the Sonatas and Symphonies until you have read Chapter X.)

3. Make up and act a little play on some incident of Mozart's life.

4. Have one or two pieces of Mozart played and then one or two pieces of Haydn, and see if you can learn to distinguish the 'flavour' of one composer from that of the other. (I wonder if you can!)

5. If you have a Gramophone at home, get your parents to buy a record of the *Figaro* Overture (or any other Mozart piece), and listen to it carefully until you know it well, and understand just how it is made up.

6. Look out for any Mozart music in the broadcast programmes and in the *Radio Times*, and when you find any, make a note of the day and time, so as not to miss it.

X

SONATAS AND SYMPHONIES

HAYDN and Mozart wrote many Sonatas and Symphonies. So did Beethoven, of whom you will learn in the next chapter. So the time has now come to tell you what Sonatas and Symphonies are like, and then you can hear lots of them and understand them.

First it must be said that a Sonata and a Symphony are one and the same thing—except that a Sonata is for one instrument, or perhaps two, whereas a Symphony is for full Orchestra (you will find a chapter on the Orchestra later).

The Sonata a sort of Suite.

In the chapter about *Music in the Days of Drake and Shakespeare* we found that composers in those days often wrote a piece that consisted of two shorter pieces put together—two dance-tune pieces, a stately one and a lively one for contrast.

Then in the chapters about Purcell and Handel and Bach we found that these composers went further and strung a good many pieces together into what we call a Suite.

Well, a Sonata (or Symphony) is like a Suite in this—it consists of three or four shorter pieces strung together to make one long one, and these pieces are so arranged as to contrast with one another. We call these shorter pieces MOVEMENTS, and say 'that Sonata has three Movements', or 'I like the first movement of that Sonata', or 'I don't care for the last movement of such and such a Symphony'.

The First Movement.

The first movement is usually the longest and most important of the Sonata or Symphony. Very often it is in a particular kind of form which we call 'Sonata Form', or (more sensibly) 'First Movement Form'. This form is made up in the following way.

First the composer takes a good tune that has come into his mind, or that he has invented, and then he takes another (in a different key, for contrast). Between these two tunes he puts a little passage, leading from the one to the other, which we call (quite sensibly this time) a BRIDGE PASSAGE. The two tunes we call FIRST SUBJECT and SECOND SUBJECT, but you will see they are not just little bits of *melody*, like Fugue Subjects, but real long tunes, with Melody, Harmony, and possibly, here and there, a bit of Counterpoint.

After the Second Subject is finished the composer generally adds a little tail-piece or CODA to round off that part of the movement. We call all this, so far, the EXPOSITION, or the ENUNCIATION, of the movement, because it 'exposes', or 'enunciates', the 'Subjects', or tunes, out of which the whole movement is to be made.

We can make a little diagram that will make the Enunciation quite clear—

ENUNCIATION OF A SONATA

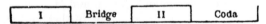

Very often the composer tells the player to repeat this Enunciation before he goes farther. The idea of this is to get the Subjects well into the listener's head, which is very important.

After the Enunciation comes a part of the Movement which we call the DEVELOPMENT. Here the composer takes a bit of one subject and works it up in various ways, and then, perhaps, a bit of the other. And he 'modulates' a great deal— that is, he takes us through many different keys, and generally excites us a good deal by doing so. It is difficult to explain how the Development is made, because it may be done in so many different ways. When you come to listen carefully to a few Sonatas, you will get to understand this.

After the Development we come to the RECAPITULATION, which is simply a repetition of the Enunciation, but with both the Subjects in the same key this time. And perhaps the composer gives us a good long Coda to finish with. So a diagram of the whole movement would look like this (you will notice that in the movement imagined here it has been supposed that the composer has given a short Introduction before the First Subject enters).

FIRST MOVEMENT OF A SONATA

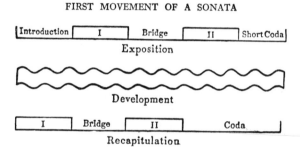

Now you understand 'Sonata Form' or 'First Movement Form', and the thing is to hear some movements that are in this form, and listen to them carefully. Sometimes second or third or last movements are in this same form and a great many Orchestral Overtures are in it, too.

The Middle Movements.

One of the middle movements is pretty sure to be a slow, expressive one, and very likely the other will be a lively MINUET AND TRIO, or a SCHERZO.

You have already learnt what a Minuet is like (page 39). The Trio is simply another Minuet, so made as to contrast with the first. After the Trio the first Minuet is repeated, so together they make 'Ternary Form' (or a 'sandwich').

Minuet	Trio	Minuet

Scherzo means 'joke', and so the Scherzo is generally a very lively, jolly movement. Sometimes it is simply a very bright Minuet.

The Last Movement.

The last movement of all is sometimes in First Movement form and sometimes in some other form. Often it is a RONDO, that is, a piece with a chief Subject that comes round and round again, perhaps like this—

I	II	I	III	I	II	I

Here there is a chief Subject (I), followed by another Subject (II), with a third Subject in the middle III (or possibly instead of III being a Subject it may be a sort of Development of the others).

Explaining Form on paper is very dull. What you really want is to hear lots of pieces and find out by using your ears how they are made. That is much more fun.

QUESTIONS

(TO SEE WHETHER YOU REMEMBER THE CHAPTER AND UNDERSTAND IT)

1. What is the difference between a Sonata and a Symphony?

2. What is the difference between a Sonata and a Suite? (This is a question that is not answered in so many words in the chapter, but you can soon think of the answer if you try.)

3. What is the word by which we call the various shorter pieces that are put together to make up a Sonata or Symphony?

4. How many of these shorter pieces generally make up the longer piece?

5. Would this be a good plan for a Symphony or Sonata?—

> Long quick piece,
> Short lively piece,
> Merry piece,
> Very rapid piece.

6. Would you prefer this?—

> Slow expressive piece,
> Funeral March,
> Solemn piece.

7. There is one dance piece often found in the Sonata and Symphony. What is it? How is it made up and what is its 'form'?

8. Describe the form often used for the first piece in the Sonata or Symphony (generally called 'Sonata Form'). How many chief tunes (or 'Subjects') does it usually have, and how are these used? What do we call the first part of the piece? What do we call the middle part? And what do we call the last part?

9. Are the two subjects when they first appear in the same key—and if not, why not? Do they ever appear in the same key in any other part of the piece?

10. What do we call those little tail-pieces that round off a piece or a section of a piece?

11. What do we call a passage that is perhaps not very important in itself but leads from one Subject to another?

12. Can you mention any differences between a Fugue Subject and a Sonata Subject?

13. What is the name for the jolly, joking sort of piece that we sometimes find as one of the middle pieces of a Sonata or Symphony?

14. Describe a Rondo of any kind.

THINGS TO DO

1. Get somebody to play you just the opening bars of each movement of a good Sonata, so that you may note the contrast between the different Movements.

2. Next get them to play the whole Sonata through, so that you can get a general idea of the Movements.

3. Next pick out the Movement you like best and find out, by listening carefully, how it is made.

4. Then do the same with all the other Movements. The great thing to do first is to find out which are the Subjects and to learn these *thoroughly*, so that you know them again wherever they occur in the piece.

5. If you play the piano find somebody else who does so and practise with him or her one or more of Haydn's Symphonies as a duet. These, of course, are really for Orchestra, but they can be got 'arranged' for Piano Duet (or Piano Solo either). Mark in pencil where the Subjects come, and study the form of the various Movements as much as you can.

6. If you have a Gramophone, get records of any Sonatas or Symphonies and listen to them over and over again, making up your mind as to which are the Subjects, and noticing where they reappear.

7. In the same way, get records of any Overtures by Mozart or Beethoven. These you will generally find are in 'Sonata Form', that is, they have only one Movement and it is like the First Movement of a Symphony.

8. Try to go to some orchestral concerts to hear Symphonies by Haydn. Look out for them, too, in the broadcast programmes.

XI

BEETHOVEN
1770–1827

How would you like to be dragged out of bed late at night so that you might have a music lesson? That was what poor little Beethoven had to put up with, and the thoughtless and unkind teacher was—*his own father*. Of course it was a good thing for little boy Beethoven that he had a parent who was a musician, but the sad part was that the father was a foolish man, and worse than that, a drunkard too. He was a singer in the choir of the Elector of Cologne, at Bonn on the Rhine.

The Young Organist.

When Beethoven was twelve years old, there came to Bonn, where he lived, a young musician called Neefe. The Elector had appointed him court organist, and he soon made use of the boy, making him his assistant. Then, too, the court theatre gave the boy an opportunity of using his talents. In those days a theatre orchestra included a 'cembalist', that is, a harpsichord player, and as Beethoven played the harpsichord and pianoforte very well, he was appointed to this important position. So I suppose he was now earning his living, and it was a good thing he was able to do so, for his father had by now become very drunken, and did little to support his family.

A Visit to Vienna.

The city of Vienna has always been one of the greatest musical centres of the world, so Beethoven longed to go there. He was seventeen before this wish was realized, and he was not able to stay long, as they sent him word that his mother was dying, and he had to hurry back.

Whilst he was at Vienna, he made one very important friend—Mozart (then about thirty years old). The elder musician was so struck with the gifts of the younger one that he gave him some lessons, and no doubt these were very valuable to him. Later he had lessons from Haydn.

Some good Friends.

But it does not do for a young musician to study nothing but music. He ought, also, to become fond of reading, and to love poetry, and pictures, and all good things. And besides that, he needs sympathy, for it is as hard for any kind of artist (poet, painter, or musician) to develop without that as for a rose-tree to bloom in a cold climate.

So it was a very happy thing that Beethoven made some good friends in Bonn, a family called von Breuning. He used to teach the children music, and the mother did all she could to help him with his general education, and to teach him good manners, and encourage him in every way.

Then there was a Count Waldstein, who became a good friend too, and in later years Beethoven dedicated to him the great piano piece which we call the 'Waldstein Sonata'.

Beethoven and the Aristocrats.

By and by Beethoven went to Vienna again, and this time he settled there. Indeed he lived there for the rest of his life. The great aristocratic people at Vienna very much admired his playing and they put aside any prejudice they had against him on account of his humble birth. Beethoven himself always thought that, since he was a musician, he was as good as any one else; he thought (and rightly, too) that it is a greater thing to be born with genius, and to cultivate it perseveringly, than to be born 'with a silver spoon in one's mouth', as people say. So he never allowed any one to snub him, but always held his own.

Holidays.

Beethoven loved nature, and when he took a holiday he would wander about the fields and woods, thoroughly happy. He wrote a Symphony called the *Pastoral Symphony*, and in that you will find that he has actually put the songs of birds and the music of the brooklet.

Some people used to stare at Beethoven in the country, because he was so wild. He would rush about and wave his arms and shout for joy.

Sometimes he was easily offended by people, and sometimes he was bad tempered. But very often his health was the cause of this, and the troubles he had to go through.

How Beethoven went Deaf.

Have you ever realized that there are some fine works of Beethoven that you can enjoy, and that he himself was never able to hear? It is so!

Deafness began before he was thirty, and it got worse and worse all the time. It is almost as sad for a musician to become deaf as for a painter to become blind.

An ungrateful Nephew.

Then Beethoven had another great trouble. He adopted a nephew who proved very unsteady and was a great anxiety to him. The love seemed to be all on the uncle's side. He worked hard to earn money to give the boy a good education, and in the end got him a commission in the army. But nothing except disappointment came from all these efforts, and the young man's behaviour was a great trouble to Beethoven.

Whenever you read anything about Beethoven being rough in his manners, or bad tempered, remember three things. *Firstly*, He was a great genius, and such a man is often irritable, because his mind is so much occupied with great big thoughts straight from heaven that he cannot help being annoyed by tiny little earthly worries. *Secondly*, He was deaf, and this often makes people suspicious. *Thirdly*, He had the great trouble with his nephew of whom I have just spoken.

But he was a warm-hearted and generous man, and is worthy of our greatest admiration.

What Beethoven wrote.

Amongst the treasures Beethoven left for us are nine Symphonies (some of them *wonderful* works) and thirty-two piano Sonatas. Then there are some Sonatas for violin and piano, and Trios and Quartets, and a Septet, and some other pieces of the kind we call 'Chamber Music'.

One Opera exists, and one only; it is called *Fidelio*. Another name it went by was *Leonora*, and the three *Leonora* Overtures and the *Fidelio* Overture, often heard at concerts, were all attempts to write an overture to the opera—one that should be really *just* the thing. They show how persevering the composer was, and how hard he found it to satisfy himself.

One of the very greatest of all his works is the Solemn Mass in D.

Beethoven adopted the same 'forms' as Haydn and Mozart (the Sonata, the Symphony, the String Quartet, and so on). But he put a greater depth of thought and of emotion into these forms. So his music, though not more beautiful than that of Haydn and Mozart, has more *meaning* in it and moves us more strongly.

QUESTIONS

(TO SEE WHETHER YOU REMEMBER THE CHAPTER
AND UNDERSTAND IT)

1. When was Beethoven born?
2. Where was Beethoven born? And where did he spend most of his life?

3. What do you know about his life as a boy?
4. Mention three of Beethoven's teachers.
5. What do you know of Beethoven's holidays?
6. What misfortunes did Beethoven have to endure?
7. When did Beethoven die?
8. Mention all the works of Beethoven you can remember.

THINGS TO DO

1. Get somebody to play you some of the shorter pieces of Beethoven, such as the Minuets and Trios or the Scherzos from his Sonatas and Symphonies, and listen carefully to find out how they are made. Make diagrams of them.

2. If you have a school Orchestra, get the conductor to teach it something of Beethoven.

3. Get your Singing Class teacher or School Choir conductor to give you something of Beethoven's to sing.

4. If possible, get hold of some book with the plot of Beethoven's opera *Fidelio*, and read it.

5. Get some pianist to play some Haydn and Mozart pieces and then some Beethoven, and see if you can feel the difference of 'flavour'.

6. If you have a Gramophone at home, get your parents to buy records of one or two Beethoven orchestral pieces, and get to know these really well.

7. Act a bit of *Fidelio* with somebody putting in some of the music at the piano, here and there, if possible.

8. Or, Act some little scene from the life of Beethoven, bringing in some of his music if possible.

9. Get up a School BEETHOVEN CONCERT, with little explanations of all the pieces read before each is performed. These little explanations should be written after you have carefully studied how the pieces are made up, and should be so written as to help the audience to understand the music. Before the programme begins (or, perhaps better, just after

the first piece), let some one read a tiny life of Beethoven, lasting about five minutes—specially written for the purpose, of course. If you like, you can intersperse the Concert with anecdotes of Beethoven, or descriptions of some special features in his life and work, each read or told by a different person, so as to bring in as many of your fellow pupils as possible.

Try to go to some orchestral concerts to hear symphonies by Beethoven. Look out for them, too, in the broadcast programmes.

XII

WHAT IS AN ORCHESTRA?

When next you see and hear an Orchestra, notice that it is a sort of small town, made up of just a few families.

The 'Scraper' Family.

Members of the family—

1st Violins. 2nd Violins. Violas. Violoncellos. (Can you spell that word?) Double-basses.

If you like you can consider the gruff Double-Bass as the father, the sweet-voiced Violoncello as the mother, the Viola as the eldest boy, and the Violins as twin girls. Notice that there is no difference between the First Violin and the Second Violin, as instruments. They have both Treble voices, but sing Treble and Alto as children often do at school. The Violas sing Tenor, the 'Cellos sing Bass, and the Double-basses sing—'double-bass'! So the stringed instruments are like a church choir or choral society, with its four voices, only they have a special party of giants, with deep voices, to sing a very low bass, underneath the other bass.

The Two 'Blower' Families.

There are two families of 'blowers'—the 'Wood-Wind' and the 'Brass'.

Wood-Wind.	*Brass.*
Flute.	Horn.
Oboe.	Trumpet.
Clarinet.	Trombone.
Bassoon.	

1. *The Wood-Wind Family.*

You all know a Flute when you see it. It is just a plain tube, blown through a hole in the side.

A PICCOLO is a small, high-pitched Flute.

The OBOE has a reed, a *double* one (two little pieces of thin wood making a small mouthpiece). It has a sweet but rather thin piercing tone. A rather bigger Oboe is called COR ANGLAIS (a very silly name, for Cor means Horn and Anglais means English, and it is neither a horn nor English).

The CLARINET has a reed, too (a *single* one), as a part of its mouthpiece. Its tone is sweet and much smoother than that of the Oboe.

Get some one to show you the Oboe player and the Clarinet player; then watch them, and try to distinguish the tone of their instruments.

The BASSOON is a sort of bass Oboe. It is too long for the player to blow it at the end, so there is a little tube coming down the side for him to put in his mouth.

2. *The Brass Family.*

The HORN is the curly instrument. It can play lovely gentle tones or hard loud ones.

The TRUMPET you all know, so why waste space telling you about it? (In some bands they have Cornets instead of Trumpets.)

The TROMBONE. When the Shah of Persia came to England they took him to hear an orchestra. He said he enjoyed two things: 'The piece the band played before the man came and waved the stick' (you know what that was) 'and the magicians who swallowed brass rods and pulled them up again.' These magicians were the Trombonists, so now you know what a Trombone is like. You have all seen their little conjuring tricks!

The TUBA is a deep bass instrument.

The 'Banger' Family.

The chief bangers are two very gentle members of the family, though they can be fierce sometimes. We call them KETTLEDRUMS. They can be tuned to particular notes, and

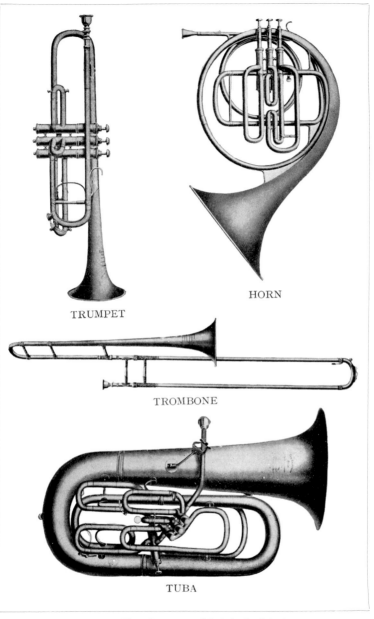

TRUMPET

HORN

TROMBONE

TUBA

The above Illustrations are not strictly proportionate in size

THE BRASS OF THE ORCHESTRA

PICCOLO

FLUTE

OBOE

COR ANGLAIS, OR ENGLISH HORN

BASSOON, or FAGOTTO

DOUBLE BASSOON or CONTRAFAGOTTO

CLARINET in B FLAT

BASS CLARINET

The above Illustrations are not strictly proportionate in size

THE WOOD-WIND OF THE ORCHESTRA

it is good fun to see the man doing this in the middle of a piece.

Two rowdy members of the family are the BIG DRUM (or Bass Drum) and the brass CYMBALS. Then there is a charming but rather brainless member who generally appears in public when merrymaking is going on—the TRIANGLE.

Warning.

If you know any players in orchestras, don't tell them that we called them 'Scrapers', 'Blowers', and 'Bangers'. They would not like it, and it is no good hurting their feelings. But that is all they really are, isn't it? Only of course they scrape, blow, and bang very artistically.

QUESTIONS

(TO SEE WHETHER YOU REMEMBER THE CHAPTER AND UNDERSTAND IT)

1. What are the four families of the Orchestra?

2. What are the members of each of these four families?

3. In the Strings, which instrument corresponds to the Trebles in a Choir? And which to the Altos? And which to the Tenors? And which to the Basses? And when you have answered those questions say whether there is any other string instrument left to be mentioned, and tell anything you can as to *its* business in life.

4. What is the difference between a Flute and an Oboe?

5. What is the difference between an Oboe and a Clarinet?

6. What is the difference between an Oboe and a Bassoon?

7. Mention the chief three Brass instruments.

8. What are the various 'Bangers' of the Orchestra called?

THINGS TO DO

1. The first 'thing to do' is to go and hear an Orchestra and to 'spot' the various instruments, so that you will know them again whenever you see them and will also know whereabouts their players usually sit in the orchestra.

2. Be there in good time and listen to the tuning-up, so as to learn what each instrument sounds like. Then keep your eye on any particular instrument and watch for its coming in, so that you may listen to its tone again.

3. Notice what the sound is like when Strings alone are playing.

4. And notice what the sound is like when Brass instruments alone are playing.

5. And, also, what the sound is like when the Wood-Winds alone are playing.

6. Keep a special eye for about a quarter of an hour on the Oboe and Clarinet, so as to catch them playing any bits of Solo, and thus learn the difference in tones so that you can tell them in the future with your eyes shut.

7. If you have a Gramophone and some orchestral records, try to discover, by listening carefully, what instruments are playing at different places in the records.

NOTE

It is a good thing at the first three or four concerts to sit very near the front, so as to be able to watch the players. After a time, when you know where all the players sit and what all the instruments sound like, you can sit farther away.

In the second volume of this book there will be given a great deal more information about Orchestras, but what is given in this volume is enough to make orchestral concerts very enjoyable if you only study it carefully and go to as many concerts as possible.

If you see a man playing any wind instrument in the street, stop and listen to him and notice what the instrument sounds like (often, as you will notice, the high notes sound very different from the low notes, so that if he were playing in an orchestra and you were not near him you would think the high passages and the low ones came from two different instruments).

XIII

ROBERT SCHUMANN
1810–1856

A School Band.

In the town academy at Zwickau in Saxony, in the year 1823, or thereabouts, there might have been seen a group of boys enjoying themselves in music after school hours. The leader of the group, young Robert Schumann, sits at the piano, and around him are grouped two violinists, two flute players, two clarinet players, and two horn players—quite a nice little band for a school, though strangely lacking in the stringed instruments, the place of which the leader has to supply on the piano so far as he can.

A great deal of happiness the boys get out of their band, and the leader looks very pleased as they play some music he has written specially for them.

Portraits in Music.

This is not the first school at which Robert has been famous for his music. At the school for younger boys, to which he went previously, he used to make great fun by playing portraits of his schoolfellows.

How can one 'play a portrait'? Well, of course, no composer, however clever, can make up a piece that will show you what a person looks like, but it is possible to give a sort of portrait of a person's character or, shall we say, temperament?

For instance, if a boy is a merry, mischievous boy, it will be possible to give some idea of this by playing merry, mischievous-sounding music. And if a boy is a solemn boy, one can play solemn music, and so forth.

That is, no doubt, what young Robert Schumann, as a boy

of ten, used to do, and he was considered to be very clever indeed at it.

Schumann the Book-lover.

There is one thing about Schumann's early life that is very important, for it seems to have influenced him as long as he lived. That thing is this—*He was brought up amongst books*.

His father was a bookseller and an author too, and so, seeing books all around him, Robert grew up a book-lover. He was especially fond of poetry and of books of a romantic kind. All this affected his music in after years, for as a composer he often pictured in music (so to speak) the characters and feelings of the people he read about, just as, when a boy, he had done the same with those of his schoolfellows. And all his music was very 'romantic', if you know what that means. You shall have a chapter later to explain the word.

It was a sad thing for Robert that his father died when he himself was only fifteen years old. The father had encouraged him not only to read books but also to study music, but the mother wished him to be a lawyer.

They try to make him a Lawyer.

By and by Robert was sent to study law at the University of Leipzig. But it was really precious little law he studied there, for he came to know a very clever piano teacher called Wieck, and spent his time having piano lessons and practising.

Weick had a little daughter named Clara, who was only half Robert's age (for she was nine and he was eighteen). She was already a very clever pianist and used to play in public with great success.

Besides practising the piano, Robert began to compose, and at last it became so clear that nature had intended him to be a musician that he was allowed to give up working at law.

'More haste, less speed.'

The trouble was that he wanted to become a great pianist too quickly, and so he used some piece of apparatus that he thought would improve his hands. But instead of this, it injured one of his hands, and he realized that he could now never become a really fine player.

This was, after all, a blessing in disguise, because it made him give himself to composition. Now if Schumann had been merely a great pianist, we to-day would have had no pleasure out of him (though our grandfathers might have done). But as he became a composer, he has given pleasure to a great many people who were born long after he died, and will give pleasure to boys and girls and men and women for long years after we, too, are dead and done for.

How Schumann edited a Paper.

In those days, as now, there were a great many people who liked frivolous, silly music, and did not appreciate music that was really beautiful. Now Schumann, having been brought up amongst books and writers, had the idea of starting a musical paper to help people to like good music. He had a little band of friends who assisted him, and their paper did a great deal of good.

Schumann used to write a great many fine articles in this paper, and whenever a brilliant young musician appeared, he did all he could, by writing about him in the paper, to encourage him and to get people to pay attention to his music.

How Schumann fought for a Wife.

As Clara Wieck grew older she and Robert Schumann realized that they were meant for each other. But old Wieck would not hear of it, as Robert was not rich, nor was he yet famous.

So there was a lawsuit about it, and Robert made the father come into court and state his reasons for refusing his consent.

When the court heard the reasons they said these were not good ones, and told Wieck that he must allow Clara to marry Robert.

So Clara and Robert were married, and happy ever afterwards—that is until a great sorrow came, of which you shall hear something in a moment.

On his marriage Schumann suddenly took to writing songs, as if to express his feelings. For a year he wrote song after song, and most of his beautiful songs were written at this time.

The Sadness of Schumann's Life.

The sad thing about Schumann's life was its ending, for he went out of his mind, and at length he had to be put in an asylum.

His nature had for some time seemed a little queer, and he often did things that struck people as odd. For instance he was very silent, and at a restaurant at Dresden he would sit night after night at a particular table, with his back to the people, just thinking quietly or working out his music in his mind.

That sort of thing did not matter much, and people only took it as one of the strange ways that genius often has. But when he became really mad every one felt very sorry, and when he died in the asylum in 1856 (aged only 46) there was great regret.

His widow gave up the rest of her life to playing the piano all over Europe to get money for her children and to make her husband's wonderful compositions known. She lived for forty years after the death of her husband.

QUESTIONS

(TO SEE WHETHER YOU REMEMBER THE CHAPTER
AND UNDERSTAND IT)

1. When and where was Schumann born, and when did he die?

2. What do you know about his music-making at school?

3. What was his father's profession, and what influence had this on him and on his music?

4. For what profession was he educated?

5. Who taught him the piano when he should have been studying law?

6. Say all you know (which should be a great deal) about this piano teacher's daughter.

7. What accident did Schumann have in trying to become a great pianist?

8. And what do you remember of his writing about music?

9. Tell something about his marriage.

10. And about his death.

THINGS TO DO

1. If you are a pianist get Schumann's *Album for the Young*, and learn some of the pieces in it. (If you are a pretty fair sight-reader you can play them without much 'learning'.) Then study how they are made and make little diagrams of some of them. Look at their titles and see if you think the music expresses the idea of the title. If you cannot play yourself, get one of your friends to play them to you, and, by listening carefully, learn all you can about them.

2. Get somebody to play you some of Schumann's bigger and harder pieces, and study them in the same way.

3. Write a little life of Schumann and paste it in your copy of the *Album for the Young* or any other music of his you possess.

4. Make and act a little play about Schumann.

5. If you have a Gramophone at home get your parents to buy some Schumann records: also look out for the name of Schumann in the broadcast programmes.

XIV

CHOPIN

1810–1849

WHEN you hear Chopin's music you must remember that its composer was half a Pole and half a Frenchman. For his father was a Frenchman and his mother a Pole.

Now the French have always been noted for writing beautifully graceful and neat music, and the Poles are very fond of wild dances, and besides this have been so much oppressed that in their music you often find something very sad or very fierce. And one or other of these various qualities, French and Polish, you generally find in the lovely piano pieces Chopin wrote.

A Boy Pianist.

When little Frederic was only nine years old he had become quite well known as a clever pianist. The rich Polish noblemen used to send for him to perform at their houses, and one day he had an invitation to take part in a great public concert.

This was the first time Frederic had performed before a large audience, and there was great excitement in the Chopin household. The little boy was dressed with great care. He stood on a chair and his mother put his best clothes on him.

There was one thing which he had never worn before, and he was very proud of it. His mother was not able to go to the concert, and when he came back she asked him, 'Well, what did the people like best?' And instead of naming one of his piano pieces the little chap exclaimed, 'Oh, Mother, everyone was looking at *my collar*!'

At this concert Frederic played a PIANOFORTE CONCERTO. This, as you probably know, is a piece in which the solo instrument, the piano, has the chief part, but a full orchestra plays too. Sometimes the piano plays alone, and sometimes the orchestra, and sometimes they both play together. To play a Piano Concerto well is a great feat.

How Frederic tamed rough people.

At that time Warsaw was ruled by the Russian Grand Duke Constantine, and he was said by everybody there to be a very violent and brutal man. But when Frederic played to him, as he often did, the Grand Duke was always as kind and gentle as possible.

But there are some people even harder to tame than Grand Dukes, and these are—*schoolboys!* Now Frederic's father had a school, and one day, when he was out, the master left in charge could not keep order.

Whilst the uproar was at its height Frederic came in and begged the boys to be quiet whilst he played them a story on the piano. Then they kept as still as mice, and the young pianist put out the lights and began to play. As he did so he told them what the music meant. It was all about robbers, who tried to get into a house with ladders, but were frightened by a noise and ran away. They came to a dark wood and lay down to sleep.

When the story got to this point Frederic played more softly until not only the robbers, but his hearers too, dropped off, one by one, to sleep.

Then he stopped playing and crept quietly out of the room to fetch his mother and sisters, so that they should have a good laugh at the sleepers. They brought lights into the room and then Frederic struck a loud chord on the piano to waken the boys.

You can imagine they all had some fun out of this incident.

Is this tale true? What do you think? Can boys be lulled to sleep as easily as that?

How he played to the Emperor of Russia, and then began to see the world.

When Frederic was fourteen the Emperor of Russia came to Warsaw. Probably the people of Warsaw were proud of their young pianist, for he was asked to play before the Emperor.

All this time Frederic had hardly been outside his native city, and it was not until he was nineteen that he began to see the world. It chanced that a professor of natural history was going to Berlin, to attend a great congress of naturalists. So it was arranged that Frederic should go with him, and that whilst the professor was attending his lectures and meetings the youth should go to concerts and the opera, and also make the acquaintance of the musicians of Berlin.

Mendelssohn, who was the same age as Chopin, and who then lived in Berlin, was present at the Congress, but Chopin did not like to introduce himself to him, because Mendelssohn had already become famous, whereas he himself was almost unknown outside his home city.

The Pianist at the Inn.

In those days travelling was, of course, done by coach, and when the professor and the young pianist came to a certain little town they stopped to change horses.

In the inn parlour Chopin found a grand piano, so he began to play. The landlord and the landlady and their daughters were delighted, and so were all the coach passengers. For some time the coach could not start, for the people would not get into it. When at last Chopin stopped playing the landlady and her daughter came to the coach after him, bringing lovely cakes to eat on the way, and wine to refresh him on the dusty road.

A Concert at Vienna.

It was now time for Frederic to be making himself known as a musician wider afield, so his father urged him to go to Vienna and give a concert there. He was then twenty.

Most of the people who heard him were delighted, but a few of the Viennese thought that he played too quietly. They were fond of loud noise. It is a good thing that Chopin did not listen to them, for his natural style, both as player and composer, was a graceful, quiet style. Sometimes his music has to be played loudly and brightly, but much of it is meant for gentle, expressive playing, and none of it is rowdy.

From Vienna Chopin went on to other capitals, such as Prague and Dresden, so now he was really seeing the world, and the world was hearing him. But for some time Vienna was his centre, to which he returned after his journeys, and where he spent many months. You will remember that this was the city where Haydn, Mozart, Beethoven, and many other composers had spent a large part of their lives. It has always been one of the most music-loving cities of the world.

How Chopin's Compositions became famous.

Some of the people at Vienna thought Chopin was a very fine pianist but not much of a composer, but gradually it became recognized that he was great in both ways.

When he composed some variations for the piano, which were published, Schumann, who, as you may remember, edited a musical paper, was so delighted with them that he wrote an article in which were the words, *Hats off, gentlemen —a Genius!*

And one day when Chopin was in the Imperial Library at Vienna, he was astonished to see a book of music there with the name of 'Chopin' on it. He said to himself, 'I have never heard of any other musician named Chopin, so perhaps there is a mistake somewhere'.

However, he took up the volume, and looked inside, and lo

and behold! it was all in his own handwriting. The publisher
of his variations had realized that the composer would one
day become famous, and, after printing the variations, had
sent the manuscript to be carefully kept for ever in the
Emperor's library.

So Chopin had a great surprise, and he wrote home to tell
his mother and father about it, and the letter can still be read.

Life in Paris.

When Chopin was twenty-two he decided to go to Paris.
There he made friends with many of the chief musicians, but
he found life very expensive, and almost decided to emigrate
to America. But one day in the street he met Prince Radzi-
will, who had been good to him when he was a boy, so he
told the Prince about the American project.

The Prince said nothing to dissuade him, but persuaded
him to come that evening to a party at the house of the great
rich Baron Rothschild. There he was, of course, asked to
play, and all the people present admired his playing so much
that he realized that the tide had turned and success was at
hand. So he never went to America after all, but stayed in
Paris and grew more and more famous.

Chopin and the Poles.

Whenever a poor Pole was in Paris, Chopin, who now
began to make lots of money, was ready to help him. Once he
had arranged to go with his friend the musician, Hiller, to the
Lower Rhine Musical Festival, which Mendelssohn was to
conduct. But when the time came he had given all his money
to some of the poor Poles who had fled to Paris for refuge,
and he had to tell Hiller to go alone.

But Hiller would not consent, and then a thought struck
Chopin. He took up the manuscript of his beautiful E flat
Waltz, ran off with it to a publisher's, and came back with
500 francs. So the two friends were able to go together after

all. At the Festival Chopin became great friends with Mendelssohn.

Chopin as a Teacher.

Chopin had a great many pupils amongst the Parisians. The chief thing that he taught them was to play with a beautiful light touch.

As you know, there are some pianists who have done lots of scales and exercises and made their fingers very strong, but who cannot play lightly. It is good for these people to practise Chopin's compositions, because many of them need to be played with a light touch, or they are spoilt.

Chopin in Britain.

All the latter part of his life poor Chopin had bad health. He was consumptive. Once he went to London especially to consult some famous doctor. He did not want people to know he was there, so he called himself Mr. Fritz. But some ladies who persuaded him to play to them guessed who it must be.

Then, in 1848, when he was thirty-eight years old, he went again. He used to be very fond of Broadwood's pianos and used to go to their shop in London to practise. But he was now so weak that, to save him exertion, someone in the shop would lift him up like a child and carry him up to the piano room.

After playing the piano a good deal at parties at some of the big houses in London, he went to Manchester, and then to Edinburgh and Glasgow. The Scottish people, who are very hospitable, almost killed him with kindness.

This visit to Britain was altogether too tiring, and Chopin went home exhausted.

The Death of Chopin.

At last, at the age of only 39, Chopin was found to be dying. One of the last things he asked for was music. He begged a Polish Countess, who had come to visit him, to sing

and play, and she did so, much to his comfort. Then, a day
or two later, he passed away.

Chopin's Music.

If you are old enough to play Chopin's music you have
perhaps already found out that he did not write many Sonatas
or other long pieces with several 'movements'. He preferred
to write shorter pieces such as Nocturnes, Preludes, Studies,
Impromptus, Ballades, Waltzes, Mazurkas, and Polonaises.

All Chopin's best music was for piano. You see this was
the instrument he loved and played so beautifully, and he
understood perhaps better than anyone who has ever lived
how to write music that should sound well on it.

QUESTIONS

(TO SEE WHETHER YOU REMEMBER THE CHAPTER AND UNDERSTAND IT)

1. What was Chopin's nationality?
2. What effect would you expect this to have on his music?
3. Tell anything you remember about the concert he
played at when nine years old?
4. What is a Pianoforte Concerto?
5. Tell a story about Chopin playing to his schoolfellows.
6. Tell a story about his playing at an inn.
7. What can you remember about Chopin's life in Vienna?
8. Why did he nearly go to America, and why did he
decide not to go after all?
9. What do you remember about his doings in Paris?
10. And what do you remember about his life in Berlin?
11. And what do you know about Chopin's style of piano
playing?
12. How did he die? And how old was he? Can you
remember any other composers who died rather young?
13. What sort of music did Chopin write?

THINGS TO DO

(FOR SCHOOL AND HOME)

1. Get somebody to play you one or two of the Nocturnes, and find out how they are made.

(*a*) What sort of work has Chopin given the right hand to do, for the most part?

(*b*) And what sort of work has he given the left hand?

(*c*) What is the 'form' of the piece? Try to make a diagram of it.

(*d*) When you have found out the form and made the diagram, find out the chief keys (if you understand keys) and put these in the diagram.

(*e*) Then see if you can find out how Chopin keeps up your interest in the piece by variety in the character of the tunes (or 'subjects') he uses, and in their keys.

(*f*) When you have done all this, have the piece played again and listen to it carefully to notice all these details.

(*g*) And finally have it played once more, without troubling much to listen to the details, but just enjoying the beauty of the piece.

2. Get someone to play you one or two of each of the following kinds of pieces by Chopin:

(*i*) **Polonaise.** As the name indicates this is a piece written in the style of a Polish national dance. It has ——[1] beats in a bar.

(*ii*) **Mazurka.** This is another Polish national dance with ——[1] beats in a bar (slower than a Valse but quicker than a Polonaise).

(*iii*) **Valse** (or Waltz). Another piece in the style of a dance. It has ——[1] beats in a bar.

3. Get somebody to play you Chopin's Berceuse. As you know, 'Berceuse' is French for Cradle Song or Lullaby.

---

[1] Listen and find out how many, and then fill up this blank for yourself.

Do you think this would be a good piece for rocking a baby to sleep? How is it made? Find out all about it by listening carefully, and then make a diagram of it. Last of all have it played again just for pleasure.

4. If possible get somebody to play you one of the Ballades and any other suitable Chopin pieces, in the same way.

5. If you have any of Chopin's music, write a little *Life of Chopin* and paste it in the beginning of the music.

6. Make up and act a little play on some incident in Chopin's life.

7. Prepare and give a little lecture on Chopin to your friends, playing, or getting some friends (young or grown-up) to play some Chopin music to illustrate it.

8. Look out for the name of Chopin in programmes in the *Radio Times* and make a note, so as not to miss the performances!

XV

WHAT IS 'ROMANTIC MUSIC'?

A Simple Explanation.

Suppose we were going through a picture gallery. We should find there were two kinds of pictures.

One kind would make us say, 'Oh, how beautiful!' We should realize that the pictures of that kind were made up by painting beautiful things, and painting them in a beautiful way. And we should get a great deal of *pleasure* from looking at them.

But we should find another kind of picture, which might, or might not, be as beautiful as the first kind, but which would make us *feel* deeply, so that we might stand in front of it and as we looked become very happy and excited, or very sad, or very awestruck, or very sympathetic.

There might, for instance, be a picture of a great admiral about to go on board his flagship in time of war. And if the artist were a very clever one we should find he had put into the brave man's face such strength of character and determination, that we ourselves should feel braver as we looked at it.

Or there might be a picture of a Sailor Boy leaving his poor old mother to go to sea, and then we should be made to feel sorrowful as we thought of the mother's sorrow, and her fears that she might never see her boy again.

Or there might be a great Battle Scene, which would stir our blood, and make us wish to fight for our country, or a picture of a Stormy Day that would make us imagine we were battling with the wind and rain, or a lovely Sunset picture that would make us feel full of awesome delight, as we do when a summer's evening ends with coloured clouds that seem to be curtains hanging before the doors of heaven.

Now the first set of pictures we might call 'Beauty Pictures', and the second sort 'Imagination Pictures'. Some of the 'Beauty Pictures' would stir the imagination a little, but their first object would be beauty, and all of the other pictures would be beautiful, more or less, but their first object would be to stir our imagination. And the second set we might call 'ROMANTIC'.

And, just in the same way, there is 'Beauty Music' and 'Imagination (or Romantic) Music'.

'Beauty Music.'

Now play over on the piano (or get someone else to play for you) a few little bits of music, the openings of three or four pieces.

Here is the beginning of one of Bach's *Inventions*:

INVENTION, BY BACH

Look at that little scrap of music carefully. It is all made out of a jolly little tune which climbs up and then runs down, given first to one hand and then to the other. If you examine the music you will see how neatly Bach has fitted things in, and the whole piece is made up just as beautifully and neatly as you will see if you get a copy of it.

Now this piece, played in a lively way, is a quite beautiful one, and we enjoy hearing it. But it does not stir our *imagination* much.

Here is the opening of another piece, the Rondo from one of Mozart's Piano Sonatas.

RONDO, BY MOZART

In this case there is a graceful tune and a simple accompaniment—but no great *imagination*.

'Imagination Music'.

Now we come to something very different. Play these bars, if your hands are big enough. They are from the opening of Beethoven's *Pathetic Sonata*.

SONATA, BY BEETHOVEN

Do you not at once feel that in this Sonata Beethoven is going to stir our feelings? This is music of quite another kind from what we have just been playing. It makes us feel solemn and awestruck. It is a piece of 'Imagination Music' or (to use the proper word) 'Romantic Music'.

Here is another Imaginative piece, of a very different kind. Play this several times and see what you think of it.

'HARLEQUIN', BY SCHUMANN

Schumann calls this piece *Harlequin*, and we feel as soon as we hear it that he has set out to make us feel we are in the midst of a party of gay revellers. Again, we have a piece of 'Romantic Music'.

And here, to close with, is a Mazurka, by Chopin.

MAZURKA, BY CHOPIN

As in the Mozart piece given above, there is a beautiful tune in the right hand and a simple accompaniment in the left. But this time the tune is not only beautiful; it is full of tender feeling. So here again is a piece of 'Romantic Music'.

The 'Romantic Composers'.

Schumann and Chopin are what are called 'Romantic Composers'. And the 'Romantic School',[1] as we call the composers who write this kind of music, grew up chiefly during the first half of last century (between 1800 and 1850). Some of the chief 'Romantic' composers are Weber, Schubert, Schumann, Chopin, Mendelssohn, and Sterndale Bennett. But much of Beethoven's music is Romantic, too (perhaps most of it, in fact), and Bach and Mozart sometimes wrote romantically, as you will find when you grow older.

[1] This doesn't mean a real School like yours, but just a *set* of Composers who wrote in something the same way as one another. We speak of a 'school of composers' just as we speak of a 'school of porpoises'.

'Romantic' Literature.

I need not tell you that, just as there are Romantic pictures and music, so there is Romantic literature. Indeed, the word really belongs to literature, though we have borrowed it for music. Any poem or tale, or description, that sets your imagination working hard, and fills you with a sense of wonder, or awe, or excitement, is Romantic. Scott's novels are 'Romances', and Shakespeare's *Midsummer-Night's Dream* and *Tempest* are very Romantic plays.

Beware!

Some people when they grow older lose the spirit of Romance, and settle down into matter-of-fact business men or anxious housewives. That is a great pity, and must not be allowed to happen to you. If the author of this book should meet you when you are *quite* old (say thirty or forty), he hopes that he will find that a beautiful country lane, or an imaginative picture, or a piece of Schumann's music, or a fairy tale, or a moving story of real life can still make you feel the thrill of *Romance*. Never let the hard blows of the world knock that out of you!

QUESTIONS

(TO SEE WHETHER YOU REMEMBER THE CHAPTER AND UNDERSTAND IT)

1. Can you describe the two sorts of pictures—and the two sorts of music?

2. Who are the chief 'Romantic Composers'?

3. About when did they live?

THINGS TO DO

1. Get somebody to play over to you a good lot of pieces (or parts of pieces) by Bach, Mozart, Beethoven, Schumann, Chopin, and the other composers mentioned in this book, and see which you think could be described as Romantic.

2. Then have them played again and see what *emotion* you think the composer has been expressing in each.

XVI

GRIEG AND HIS NORWEGIAN MUSIC
1843–1907

A LITTLE Norwegian boy of five stood before his mother's piano. The lid was open and he was looking at the keys from which his mother got such wonderful sounds every day. He thought he too would like to make music.

So, as he stood there, he timidly put down a note, .

That sounded all right, but what he liked, when his mother played, was the sound of several notes played together, so he tried to find another to go with the first. And this was what

he found: ♮. That he thought was lovely, and he played it quite a lot of times for the pleasure of hearing it:

Then he began to wonder whether he could find a third note to go with these two, and, by and by, he discovered

this: ♮. Then he began to get excited. Could he find a fourth? He tried:

but that would not do (try it yourself and see). So then he tried:

and that made him very happy. His eyes sparkled with joy. He had found four notes that sounded beautiful when they were played together.

Now he became really ambitious. He wanted to find still another note, to make five altogether. His little fingers felt about on the keys and he got this chord:

Years after, when Edward Grieg was a very famous man, he was asked what was the first success of his life. And, in reply, he did not tell of the first piece of music of his that was ever published, or the first concert at which he played, but of finding that simple chord (which we call the 'chord of the ninth') when he was a little boy of five. That childish discovery had given him as much pleasure as anything he ever did in his life.

A great deal of the charm of modern music lies in what we call 'harmony' (that is, as you know, putting notes together so that they sound beautiful with one another), and Grieg, when he was a man, was to become famous for his lovely 'harmonies'. So it is not surprising to learn that he had an 'instinct' for 'harmony', even when he was only a little chap of five.

The First Music Lessons.

Now as we all know (only we don't like to talk about it), some children (though of course not many) are—*lazy*! But it is a consolation to know that even the laziest children sometimes grow out of their laziness and become useful people in the world, and that even great men were often lazy little boys.

So it was with Grieg. When his mother, who was a good player, began to give him piano lessons, a year later than the incident I have just related, he was at first delighted, but when he found that it meant *Practice*—then he felt sad. You see a good deal of what we have to practise, if we want to become good pianists, has not much music in it. We soon get tired of this little tune, don't we?—

And even this longer tune—

is not very exciting!

But Grieg's mother said that he must practise these tunes, and other tunes no better, or he would never become a good player, and instead of letting him sit down at the piano making up little tunes of his own and finding fresh chords, she kept him at the drudgery. Grieg liked to *dream*, and his mother wanted him to *do*. So there was sometimes trouble. But the mother's will was stronger than the child's, and so little Edward began to make progress.

School Days.

When he went to school it was the same thing. He did not at all like the hard work. Here is a little tale he tells of an arithmetic lesson.

The teacher said there should be some little reward for the first to get a sum right.

Now Grieg had a brilliant idea. He thought ' "o" means nothing; if I leave out all the noughts, it will save time in reckoning and make no difference to the answer'. So, as he added, or multiplied, or divided, whenever there came a nought he just left it out. That, he thought, was a short cut to success. But he didn't get the prize!

When he made a mistake in the English lesson Grieg's master made great sport about it, because Grieg's father was the British Consul at Bergen. And then the boy went red and felt ashamed of himself, and very unhappy.

The boys were unjust, too. I do not know whether you have ever noticed it, but children at school are often very cruel. One day, in the reading lesson, they came to the word 'Requiem', and the master asked if any of them knew what great composer had written a piece of church music with that name. Grieg answered 'Mozart', and as he was the only one who knew, the other boys were jealous and started calling him 'Mozak', and shouting it after him in the streets. That, as you will admit, was both foolish and unfair.

The Singing Class.

In the singing class Grieg could always do well. One day the master asked them about the scales and their sharps and flats, and Grieg was the only one who knew them. Now the singing master was a nice, kind man (as, of course, all music-teachers are!) and he gave Grieg such warm praise that it encouraged him for weeks after, and made him feel a little more self-confident.

A Piece of Good Luck.

For a time Grieg was not very well, and had to stay away from school. He thought he was going to make a holiday of it, but his father did not mean him to be idle and kept him at work. In particular he made him learn by heart the history of the French king, Louis XIV. This was a bitter task, but it had to be done, and the father was not satisfied until every word in the chapter was known.

One day when Grieg had returned to school, the teacher said he would examine the boys in history. Here is Grieg's own description of what happened:

'The teacher sat as usual, and balanced himself on one leg of his chair, while he turned over the leaves backwards and forwards, considering where he could catch me best. A long and painful silence. At last he came out with: "Tell me something about Louis XIV". It poured out as from a barrel with the bung out. Unceasingly flowed the stream of my speech. Not a word was left out. It was all as if nailed to my memory. The teacher was dumb with astonishment. He tried not to believe his ears; but the facts had spoken. There was nothing more to bring against me.

'Once more a turning over of the leaves, once more a wriggle on the leg of the chair. The sweat of anxiety burst from my forehead. It was impossible that for the second time I should be more lucky than wise. But my good star did not forsake me. "Can you tell me what Admirals were on the Black Sea under Catherine II?" With a loud voice I answered, "Admirals Greigh and Elphinstone".

'Those names had been welded into my consciousness ever since my father had told me that our family arms, which bore a ship, denoted that our original ancestor was, in all probability, the Scotch Admiral Greigh. The teacher clapped the book to. "Quite right; for that you will get a 'one' and a star."

'I was as proud as a Field-Marshal after a victory. I almost think that was the greatest success of my school life. All the greater shame to me that its real meaning was so small!'

Grieg's First Musical Composition.

The next incident related shows that Grieg's lucky star was not perpetually shining. One day he brought to school a music-book on which he had written in large letters:

VARIATIONS ON A GERMAN MELODY BY EDWARD GRIEG. OPUS 1.

This he showed to a schoolfellow, who, however, took so lively an interest in the composition as to attract the teacher's attention. This personage insisted on knowing what was the matter, and at last was told, 'Grieg has composed something'.

'The teacher came to me, looked at the music-book, and said in a peculiar, ironical tone: "So the lad is musical, the lad composes. Remarkable!" Then he opened the door into the next class-room, fetched the teacher in from there, and said to him: "Here is something to look at. This little urchin is a composer!"

'Both teachers turned over the pages of the music-book with interest. Every one stood up in both classes. I felt sure of a grand success. But that is what one should never feel too quickly. For the other teacher had no sooner gone away than my master suddenly changed his tactics, seized me by the hair till my eyes were black, and said gruffly: "Another time he will bring the German Dictionary with him, as is proper, and leave this stupid stuff at home." Alas to be so near the summit of fortune, and then, all at once, to see oneself plunged into the depths! How often that has happened to me in later life! And I have always been driven to remember the first time.'

The Friendly Lieutenant.

Opposite the school there lived a young lieutenant who was fond of music, and a good pianist. Grieg came to know him, and used to take his attempts at composition to show him.

The kind lieutenant, unlike the harsh schoolmaster, was always interested, and used to ask Grieg to make him copies of everything. All Grieg's life through he remembered this lieutenant, and felt grateful to him for his encouragement, and when, step by step, his friend rose to be a general, he felt very pleased indeed.

The Story of Ole Bull, and Grieg's going to Leipzig.

There was at that time a very famous Norwegian violinist called Ole Bull. He was a very adventurous man and went all over the world playing his violin to big audiences everywhere. Especially he loved to play the old Norwegian folk-tunes. Grieg had often heard his father and mother talk of this wonderful man. One summer's day, when he was nearly fifteen, he saw a rider on a fine Arab horse dashing up the road from Bergen. When he reached the Griegs' gate, he stopped and jumped off. It was the celebrated Ole Bull, and he had come to visit them.

First he told them jokes and wonderful tales of his adventures in America. Then he made Grieg go to the piano, and, when he had heard him play some of his own boyish compositions, he became serious, and talked quietly to the parents.

Then he came over to Grieg and said, 'It is all arranged. You are to go to Leipzig and become a musician'.

That was a great day for Grieg!

So across the North Sea to Hamburg went young Edward. And very lonely he felt when at last he was deposited in a boarding-house at Leipzig, with no one around him who could speak a word of his native Norwegian.

Grieg and the Peasants.

As the readers of this book are young people, this chapter is chiefly about Grieg's younger days. But it is necessary to tell just a few very important things about him when he grew up.

One thing you ought to know is that Grieg was a very patriotic Norwegian. He loved his native country, and though he was trained in music largely in Germany, he tried to write real *Norwegian Music*.

You already know that country people, who have never had music lessons, nevertheless possess beautiful songs that are handed down from generation to generation. Grieg was very fond of the Folk-Songs of Norway, and used to love to hear the peasants singing them. And, whenever he could, he would get the country fiddlers to play him some of their jolly Folk-Dance music.

What Grieg wrote.

Grieg wrote a great deal of music for the piano—far more than most people know, for nearly every pianist plays the same few pieces instead of getting to know all of them.

Then he wrote a very fine Piano Concerto. He also wrote a lot of music for a lovely play by the Norwegian writer, Ibsen. This play is called *Peer Gynt*. Some of the music for *Peer Gynt* he also arranged in such a way that orchestras could play it as concert music, and it is in two 'Suites' or sets of pieces, called the *'Peer Gynt' Suites*. You can get these for piano solo or duet if you like, and very beautiful they are.

Many charming songs are amongst Grieg's works. His wife (who was also his cousin, by the way) was a beautiful singer, and sometimes the pair would go to England (of which country they were very fond), and Mrs. Grieg would give Song Recitals of her husband's songs, with the composer as accompanist.

There are also three sonatas for Piano and Violin and one for Piano and 'Cello. Altogether Grieg left us a lot of charming music, and all young musicians should look forward to playing more and more of it as they grow older.

QUESTIONS

(TO SEE WHETHER YOU REMEMBER THE CHAPTER
AND UNDERSTAND IT)

1. When was Grieg born? When did he die?
2. Tell the story of his first experiment in harmony.
3. Did he like his music lessons? Do you like yours?
4. Tell any tales you remember about his schoolwork—arithmetic, history, singing class, and so on.
5. Tell about the teacher who discouraged his composing and the soldier who cheered him.
6. Who was Ole Bull, and what did he do for Grieg?
7. What was Grieg's nationality, and how did this affect his music?
8. Mention any music Grieg wrote.

THINGS TO DO

1. If you are a pianist ask your teacher for some of the Grieg pieces such as you can play (perhaps one or two of the *Lyric Pieces*).
2. If you are a pretty good player get the *Peer Gynt* suite, arranged for Piano Solo or Duet, or some of the other music so arranged, and practise it.
3. If you have a Gramophone get your parents to buy some Grieg records: there are some good ones.
(Whatever you do, mind you study how the pieces you play on Piano or Gramophone are made, and notice as much as you can about them.)
4. If you are a pretty good pianist get Grieg's *Four Norwegian Dances* (Op. 35) for Piano Duet, and play them with a friend. They are *very* jolly music.
5. Get somebody to play to you as much Grieg music as possible, and study how it is made. Make diagrams of it.

Notice any Norwegian peculiarities. You can soon find out what they are, for they will strike you as quite different from anything you have heard in the English, German, Austrian, Polish, and French music previously studied.

6. If you have some of Grieg's music, write a little *Life of Grieg* and paste it at the beginning.

7. Make a little play of Grieg, and act it with your friends.

8. Look out for the name of Grieg in programmes in *The Radio Times* and make a note, so as not to miss the performances!

XVII

EDWARD ELGAR

1857–1934

You know, I suppose, that Elgar was born into a very musical family. His father was an organist and music-seller in Worcester. If you go to that city you can still see the shop where Elgar's father lived and did his business and where Elgar himself was born.

Elgar's First Music Lesson.

Living amongst music as he did, little Edward soon began to think he would like to be a music maker. He was only five years old, and of course, did not understand things very well, but he noticed that when people played or sang they had a piece of paper before them with lines ruled on it, and black marks for the notes. So he got a piece of paper and ruled some lines and began to compose a grand piece.

It was a bright warm spring day, so he went outside to do his work, and sat down at the side of the house. He thought he was writing something very fine indeed and sat there absorbed in his work, lost to everything going on around him.

Now whilst little Elgar, the musician, was composing his music, a house-painter was at work near him. The painter saw the little boy sitting there below, and wondered what he was doing so intently. By and by he came down his ladder and looked over the child's shoulder. 'Why!' he exclaimed, 'your music has only got four lines to each stave. Music always has five lines!'

That was the first music lesson Elgar had.

A Musical Home.

As has been said, music was all around Elgar when he was a little boy. On Sundays he heard his father play the organ at St. George's Roman Catholic Church, and during the week people were coming into the shop all day to buy songs and piano pieces, and, of course, talking to his father about the music they wanted to buy. Nearly all the conversation, as the family sat at meals, was about music. Music seemed the most natural thing in life to that family—just as natural as eating and drinking.

Now that is a very important thing to remember. As you have read the lives of various great musicians in this book you must have noticed that most of them were brought up in a musical 'atmosphere'—they 'breathed' music, so to speak. Many of them had musical homes, where they heard music from their earliest years. Others became choir boys, and so were brought up amongst music. Of course there are some exceptions to this (as, for instance, Handel), but generally it was so. And certainly in Elgar's case we owe a great deal to the fact that the household in which he was born and in which he lived was a musical one.

A Great Event.

But though little Edward Elgar lived amongst music and took an interest in it, and learnt a great deal about it almost without knowing he was doing so, it was one particular event which occurred that really roused him. He once told the present writer all about it, and here it is.

One day, as he was looking at some of the music in his father's shop, he came across Beethoven's First Symphony. (Beethoven wrote nine symphonies, as you already know.)

Now the First Symphony is, naturally, the simplest of all

THE MAGIC MUSIC THAT AWAKENED
ELGAR

Allegro Molto e Vivace.

Reproduced by kind permission of Messrs. Augener, Limited.

the nine. But it has a Scherzo that when it was written must have astonished people very much by its rapid modulations.

And as Elgar looked at the first page of this Scherzo, he suddenly felt on fire with excitement. He had never seen such a piece before, and rushed off with the book under his arm to study it in quietness. With six children about it a house is rather noisy, as some of you may have experienced, but Elgar found a quiet place outside, and there he stayed reading this marvellous music through, over and over again, and taking in its harmonies and modulations.

If you look carefully at the page of music given, you will find it begins in key C, but 'modulates' by the time it gets to the double bar into key G. Then comes a modulation into E♭, followed by one into C minor. A♭ follows, and before long it is in D♭. As those of you who know something of the theory of music will agree, it has now travelled a very long way in a very short time. These modulations are very 'romantic'. When the piece is well played they make you feel quite excited. You will see that Beethoven inspired Elgar, and perhaps in future times it will be recorded that Elgar inspired you or some other boy or girl. For music is like measles in one way: it is 'catching'!

The Instruments Elgar played.

Now that Elgar had become really 'keen' about music he began to teach himself to play all the instruments on which he could lay hands. He became a pianist, and in later years had a good reputation about Worcester as an accompanist. He played the organ, too, and was able to take his father's place at the church, when necessary. The violoncello and the double-bass he also played pretty well, and when the orchestral society gave a symphony by Mozart or Haydn, he would play one of these instruments.

Then, too, Elgar learnt to play the bassoon, and with four friends made up a quintet.

Elgar as Violinist.

But Elgar's chief instrument was the violin. He worked hard at this and became a very good player. And for years to come he was known not as a composer but as a violinist.

One of the finest works Elgar ever wrote is a Violin Concerto. If ever you have a chance be sure to hear this. When you do so you will realize that it is a work that could never have been written by any composer who had not been a violinist. All the powers of the violin are used in it, and it is perhaps the most difficult violin piece ever written.

Studies in Theory.

Besides studying these various instruments, Elgar worked at the theory of music. You must remember that his success is not due merely to his being born with musical 'genius', and brought up in a musical 'atmosphere', but also to his having lots of perseverance. He really *tried*.

When he was talking to the present writer about his early life he showed him a parcel of his early studies that had just been found at Worcester and sent to him. There was sheet after sheet of music paper, with the exercises he had worked, and the attempts at composition he had made. You see a great composer has to *work*, just as you have to do. If a boy wants to be a good pianist he has to toil at his exercises and scales, and if he wants to be a composer he has to struggle with his harmony and counterpoint.

From Mozart to Elgar.

It is rather interesting to know that Elgar was a sort of musical descendant of Mozart. Mozart had a friend and pupil called Michael Kelly—an Irishman. And Kelly had a pupil called Sutton (a Dover man), and Elgar's father learnt music from Sutton, and Elgar naturally learnt a good deal of music from his father. Thus we may see that, in a musical way, Elgar is a great-great-grandson of Mozart, which is an

I*1

interesting little fact to remember—and one of which he was proud.

Elgar's Works.

The list of Elgar's works is a very long one. Besides a great many shorter pieces, such as songs and part-songs, and violin solos, it includes the oratorios, *The Dream of Gerontius*, *The Apostles* and *The Kingdom*, the fine *Enigma Variations* for Orchestra, two Symphonies, a Violin Concerto, a 'Cello Concerto, and some Chamber music.[1]

QUESTIONS

(TO SEE WHETHER YOU REMEMBER THE CHAPTER
AND UNDERSTAND IT)

1. When and where was Elgar born?

2. Tell anything you remember about his home.

3. What piece of music really woke Elgar up to the wonders of music, and how did it do this?

4. What instruments did Elgar learn to play? Which was the chief one?

5. Give the names of any pieces of Elgar.

THINGS TO DO

1. Get somebody to play you one of the *Pomp and Circumstance* Marches, or get it played on the Gramophone. Listen to it carefully and find out how a military march is made (these marches were written specially for the British Army). Make a diagram.

2. If you have a Gramophone get your parents to buy one

[1] By 'Chamber Music' we mean such music as String Quartets and other pieces for two or more instruments, such as are meant rather for people to play together in a room (or chamber) than for public performers to play in great concert halls.

or two of the Elgar songs—particularly those from the children's play, *The Starlight Express*.

3. Play or get somebody to play, or perform on the Gramophone, *The Wild Bear*, *The Tame Bear*, and the other pieces from *The Wand of Youth* suite. Find out how these pieces are made and make diagrams of them. Also discuss with your friends what is the idea of each piece as suggested to you by its title, and consider whether this idea is successfully carried out.

4. If you have any of Elgar's music write a little Life of Elgar and paste it in.

5. Make up and act a little play about Elgar as a boy.

6. Play or get somebody to play you the piece which 'awakened' Elgar, and try to find out what it was that stirred him so much.

7. Look out for the name of Elgar in programmes in *The Radio Times* and make a note, so as not to miss the performances!

XVIII

MACDOWELL—THE AMERICAN COMPOSER

1861–1908

THIS is the only chapter in the book about an American composer. Why is that? Well, the fact is that America has not yet had a great many really big composers, though she may soon have more. How does that come about? Why should Russia and France and Germany and Austria and Italy and Britain have long lists of great composers, and America only a short list—and that without many names of world-wide fame?

A New Country.

The reason is a simple one. America is still a *new country*. Of course we know that Europeans settled in America long since. The Pilgrim Fathers landed from their little 'Mayflower' boat in 1620—over three hundred years ago. But, in the history of a country, three hundred years is a very short time.

Just think for a moment of those Pilgrim Fathers landing at the place they called Plymouth Rock, on the rough Atlantic coast. What a desert place they found! At first they were so busy in trying to get food and to make shelter for themselves that we may be sure they thought little about music. They had to grow crops and kill wild animals, defend themselves against the fiercer Indian tribes and make friends with the more kindly ones—and all this gave them enough to do!

The Music of the Pilgrim Fathers.

Of course even busy people have some music, and so had these Pilgrim Fathers. They had no orchestras, nor string quartets, nor harpsichords, nor organs, but in their simple Sabbath worship they had the singing of Psalms to some of the old tunes they had learnt in England.

These brave men and women had with them some copies of a book of psalm-tunes which had been printed for them in Amsterdam at the time they were taking refuge in Holland, before they came to America, and they had other psalm-books which had been printed in England for use in church services there.

By and by, only twenty years after they landed, they even printed a psalm-book of their own, generally called to-day *The Bay Psalm-Book*. This was a very famous book, so much so that in England and Scotland also people printed and sold copies of it. Thus the Pilgrims were giving back to the old country they had come from some of the old tunes they had brought with them from it.

So the Puritans who went to America loved psalm music: tunes like the 'Old Hundredth', for instance, they sang heartily. But it was not to be expected that their music should get much beyond this for some time. It is generally understood that no organ was ever seen in America until 1741, one hundred and twenty-one years after the Pilgrims landed. And as for music out of church they cannot have had a great deal.

No Orchestras nor Organs in America in those days.

You see that while music is a *necessity*, it is also a *luxury*. Everywhere in the world people have music. If people are to have such things as great organs and orchestras and sonatas and symphonies they must live in towns and cities, and must be rich enough to pay for the music they enjoy.

If you went to Central Africa to-day you could sing songs

and hymns there, and get others to join you, but you could not get up an orchestra, could you? And so you could never perform a Symphony. And you could not find amongst your companions a composer to write beautiful Piano Sonatas, because all your companions would be busy growing crops and shooting lions and building bungalows. Very likely you would have to wait fifty years before you could have any *elaborate* music, and it might be two or three hundred years before the settlement you had founded could produce a great composer.

Music in America to-day.

So it was with America. But as the country became dotted with towns, more and more music was heard, and now in America you will hear fine big organs, well played by famous American organists, and piano recitals by American pianists, and orchestral concerts given by magnificent orchestras in such cities as New York, Boston, and Chicago. And nowadays there are quite a lot of American composers, though, as has been said, few really *great* ones as yet. By great, we mean, of course, in the sense that Byrd and Bach and Beethoven are great.

The greatest American Composer.

Most people think that the greatest composer America has yet produced is Edward Macdowell. Perhaps you will think that must be a Scottish name, and so it is, for Macdowell had Scots blood in him.

There have been other fine American composers during the last sixty years, but Macdowell has given us the greatest amount of fine music, and if you are a musician you ought to know something about him and, still more, know some of his music. Most of it is of such a kind that young folks can easily understand it, and some of it you will really love as soon as you hear it.

Macdowell's Boyhood.

It will not take long to tell about Macdowell's life, for it had no great adventures.

He was born in New York (what date—do you remember?). As he was so fond of music his parents allowed him to have lessons from the best pianists to be found there.

When he was fifteen the boy came to Europe to continue his studies. First he went to Paris and studied in the Conservatoire there. Then he went to Wiesbaden, in Germany, and worked hard under some of the most famous teachers of piano and composition, especially one called Raff (whose *Cavatina* some of you have heard).

He becomes a Teacher and University Professor.

After this he began teaching—though of course, like all great men, he continued learning until the end of his life. He became the chief piano teacher at the Conservatoire at Darmstadt, and also taught in other German cities. He was very fond of England and Scotland, and often visited them.

When he was twenty-seven Macdowell returned to America. He went to Boston and became well known as a fine pianist and teacher of piano. Then the great Columbia University, in New York, invited him to become its Professor of Music, and unfortunately he said he would go.

Why 'unfortunately'? Well, you see, Providence had meant him to be a Pianist and a Composer—*not* a Professor, and the work of preparing lectures and teaching classes was not good for him. He had lots of worries, and this prevented him from composing as much as he ought to have done. So it is a pity he ever went to the University.

After eight years at Columbia he gave up his post and then, sad to say, his brain gave way.

Now it is a sorrowful thing when a clever man dies, but perhaps it is even more sorrowful to see him still living but without his full reason. However, Macdowell's weakness was a rather beautiful sort of weakness, for he did not become mad but simply, as it were, a child again. He would sit in his chair for hours and play with gold pieces, or quietly amuse himself in some other way.

Mrs. Macdowell.

Do you remember that in the Grieg chapter you were told about Mrs. Grieg, and in the Schumann chapter about Mrs. Schumann? Grieg was very happy in his wife, because she was a musician and a great help and comfort to him, and just the same was the case with Schumann.

So it was also with Macdowell. He married one of his pupils, and she was able to appreciate his musical gifts and help him in his work, and, after his death, to carry on his work by playing his compositions everywhere up and down America.

Macdowell's Music.

Macdowell invented a new term to describe his works. He called it 'Suggestive' music.

You know that there is a great deal of beautiful music that we love to hear because it is beautiful, but that does not suggest any particular thoughts to us. But there is other music which is also beautiful and which reminds us of brooklets or mountains, or fairies, or fighting—as the case may be. Perhaps the composer had one of these things in his mind when he wrote the piece; and when you hear the piece the same thought probably comes to you. That is what Macdowell meant by 'Suggestive Music'. It is a sort of Romantic Music.

If you look at the titles of Macdowell's piano pieces you will see such titles as *Elfin Dance*, or *March Wind*, or *To a Wild Rose*, or *Will o' the Wisp*, or *From a Deserted Farm*, or '*MDCXX*'.

All these show that when Macdowell wrote music he was not merely trying to write down beautiful sounds, but also trying to put into the sounds some of the charming thoughts that were always passing through his mind. He was a very *imaginative* man, and another name for his music would be 'Imaginative Music'. You can call it that if you like.

By the way, what does that title '*MDCXX*' mean? Isn't that a strange title for a piece—just a date and nothing else? What date is it? If you do not remember, look through the earlier part of this chapter and see if anything there reminds you. Then get someone to play you this piece and see what 'suggestion' it makes to you. Use your imagination as you hear it, and you will enjoy it all the more.

QUESTIONS

(TO SEE WHETHER YOU REMEMBER THE CHAPTER AND UNDERSTAND IT)

1. What do you think is the reason that there have not yet been a great many *big* American composers?

2. When did the Pilgrim Fathers land, and what sort of music did they have?

3. Why do we not find great composers in new countries?

4. When was Macdowell born and where?

5. Where did he study piano-playing?

6. And where did he teach the piano?

7. When he returned to America where did he settle first—and where next?

8. Tell anything you remember about his last years.

9. Do you remember anything about Mrs. Macdowell?

10. How did Macdowell describe his music, and what did he mean by the description?

THINGS TO DO

1. If possible get somebody to play you Macdowell's piece called MDCXX (in the *Sea Pieces*) and see what impression

it gives you. Can you feel the sea? Do you get any impression in any part of it of the Puritan psalm-singing? Do you think the composer has succeeded in giving a picture of Puritan courage and sincerity?

After thinking about these things study how the piece is made and make a diagram if you can (it is a rather hard piece to make a diagram of, perhaps). Then try to find out how Macdowell got the effect of the sea into his music.

2. Get somebody to play you other pieces by Macdowell and study them in the same way. There are lots of short pieces which are very beautiful and each of them 'suggests' something. Ask yourself what it suggests and then study how it is made up and how the 'suggestion' is conveyed. I do not think that there is any composer mentioned in this book whose pieces you will like better than those of Macdowell. Many of them are just the thing for young listeners. You would, for instance, like the rather humorous pieces, called *Marionettes*, the *Woodland Sketches*, the various *Sea Pieces*, the *Fireside Tales* (especially 'Brer Rabbit'), and some of the *New England Idyls*.